# STICK FLY

# STICK FLY

### ⊰A PLAY⊱

## LYDIA R. DIAMOND

NORTHWESTERN UNIVERSITY PRESS

EVANSTON, ILLINOIS

Northwestern University Press
www.nupress.northwestern.edu

Printed in the United States of America

10 9 8 7 6 5 4 3

LIBRARY OF CONGRESS
CATALOGING-IN-PUBLICATION DATA

Diamond, Lydia R., 1969–
  Stick fly : a play / Lydia R. Diamond.
  p. cm.
  ISBN 978-0-8101-2535-3 (pbk. : alk.
paper)
  1. African American families—
Drama. I. Title.
PS3604.I1557S75 2008
812.6—dc22
                          2008027954

All photographs copyright © Michael Bros-
ilow; taken at the Congo Square Theatre
Company production.

## PRODUCTION HISTORY

*Stick Fly* was developed in part at Chicago Dramatists and premiered on March 23, 2006, as a presentation of Congo Square Theatre Company (Derrick Sanders, Artistic Director) in Chicago, Illinois, with the following cast:

Taylor . . . . . . . . . . . . . . . . . . . . . . . . . . . . . . . . . . . . . . . . Ann Joseph
Kent . . . . . . . . . . . . . . . . . . . . . . . . . . . . . . . . . . . . . . Daniel J. Bryant
Cheryl . . . . . . . . . . . . . . . . . . . . . . . . . . . . . . . . . . . Ericka Ratcliff
Flip . . . . . . . . . . . . . . . . . . . . . . . . . . . . . . . . . . . Aaron Todd Douglas
Dad . . . . . . . . . . . . . . . . . . . . . . . . . . . . . . Phillip Edward Van Lear
Kimber . . . . . . . . . . . . . . . . . . . . . . . . . . . . . . . . . . . . . Anne Roche

Director . . . . . . . . . . . . . . . . . . . . . . . . . . . . . . . . . . . . Chuck Smith
Set Design . . . . . . . . . . . . . . . . . . . . . . . . . . . . . . . . . Dustin Efird
Costume Design . . . . . . . . . . . . . . . . . . . . . . . . . . Christine Pascual
Lighting Design . . . . . . . . . . . . . . . . . . . . . . . . . . . . . . Alex Seiler
Sound Design . . . . . . . . . . . . . . . . . . . . . . . . . . . . . . Joe Plummer
Properties Design . . . . . . . . . . . . . . . . . . . . . . . . . Joanna Iwanicka
Stage Manager . . . . . . . . . . . . . . . . . . . . . . . . Edward D. Richardson
Supervising Lighting Design . . . . . . . . . . . . . . . . . . . Benny Gomes
Dramaturge . . . . . . . . . . . . . . . . . . . . . . . . . . . . . Lenora Inez Brown

The Congo Square Theatre production ran from March 23, 2006, to April 15, 2006.

*Stick Fly* was subsequently produced by True Colors Theatre Company (May 19, 2007, through June 3, 2007) with the following cast:

Taylor . . . . . . . . . . . . . . . . . . . . . . . . . . . . . . . . . . . JeNie Fleming
Kent . . . . . . . . . . . . . . . . . . . . . . . . . . . . . . . . . . . . . Jahi Kearse
Cheryl . . . . . . . . . . . . . . . . . . . . . . . . . . . . . . . Ayesha Ngaujah

Flip . . . . . . . . . . . . . . . . . . . . . . . . . . . . . . . . . . . . . . . . Javon Johnson
Dad . . . . . . . . . . . . . . . . . . . . . . . . . . . . . . . . . . . . . Greg Alan Williams
Kimber . . . . . . . . . . . . . . . . . . . . . . . . . . . . . . Elizabeth Wells Berkes

Director . . . . . . . . . . . . . . . . . . . . . . . . . . . . . . . . . . Derrick Sanders
Artistic Director . . . . . . . . . . . . . . . . . . . . . . . . . . . . . . . Kenny Leon
Managing Director . . . . . . . . . . . . . . . . . . . . . . . . . . . . Jane Bishop
Production Manager . . . . . . . . . . . . . . . . . . . . . . . . . Lisa L. Watson
Stage Manager . . . . . . . . . . . . . . . . . . . . . . . . . Joan Foster McCarty
Set Design . . . . . . . . . . . . . . . . . . . . . . . . . . . . . . . Rochelle Barker
Costume Design . . . . . . . . . . . . . . . . . . . . . . . . . . . Shilla Benning
Lighting Design . . . . . . . . . . . . . . . . . . . . . . . . . . . . . Jessica Coale
Sound Design . . . . . . . . . . . . . . . . . . . . . . . . . . . . Chris Bartelski

*Stick Fly* was also produced by the McCarter Theatre Company (September 14, 2007, through October 14, 2007), with the first preview on September 7, 2007, and the following cast:

Taylor . . . . . . . . . . . . . . . . . . . . . . . . . . . . . . Michole Briana White
Kent . . . . . . . . . . . . . . . . . . . . . . . . . . . . . . . . . . . . . Kevin Carroll
Cheryl . . . . . . . . . . . . . . . . . . . . . . . . . . . . . . . Julia Pace Mitchell
Flip . . . . . . . . . . . . . . . . . . . . . . . . . . . . . . . . . . . . . Javon Johnson
Dad . . . . . . . . . . . . . . . . . . . . . . . . . . . . . . . . . . . . . . John Wesley
Kimber . . . . . . . . . . . . . . . . . . . . . . . . . . . . . . Monette Magrath

Director . . . . . . . . . . . . . . . . . . . . . . . . . . . . . . Shirley Jo Finney
Artistic Director . . . . . . . . . . . . . . . . . . . . . . . . . . . . Emily Mann
Company Manager . . . . . . . . . . . . . . . . . . . . . . . . . . . . Jeff Price
Production Manager . . . . . . . . . . . . . . . . . . . . . . . . . Cheryl Mintz
Stage Manager . . . . . . . . . . . . . . . . . . . . . . . . . . . . Alison Cote
Set Design . . . . . . . . . . . . . . . . . . . . . . . . . . . Felix E. Chochren
Costume Design . . . . . . . . . . . . . . . . . . . . . . . . . . . Karen Perry
Lighting Design . . . . . . . . . . . . . . . . . . . . . . . . . . . . Victor Tan
Sound Design . . . . . . . . . . . . . . . . . . . . . . . . . . . Darron L. West

# STICK FLY

# CHARACTERS

*Taylor*, twenty-seven, daughter from an earlier marriage of renowned public intellectual James Bradley Scott. She was raised by a single-mother college professor. Although she carries his name, and so has had entrée to some social privileges, her father was not a part of her life. She also has gone without financially.

*Kent (Spoon)*, thirty-one, youngest son of the LeVay family. He has grown up with an artistic disposition in a family of doctors and lawyers. Although financially privileged, he has struggled to find his place in life and with his family. He loves Taylor, and though she may not see it, his gentleness is a valuable ingredient in their relationship.

*Cheryl*, eighteen to twenty-two, daughter of the family maid. Pretty, bright, always well intentioned, she has always had a crush on Flip.

*Flip (Harold LeVay)*, thirty-six, oldest son of the LeVay family. The "golden boy" who, with some compromises, has fallen in line with his father's expectations. He is an incorrigible ladies' man.

*Dad (Joe LeVay)*, fifty-eight to sixty-two, LeVay patriarch. A well-intentioned man who rules his family with a firm, loving hand. He, like Flip, has always had a way with women.

*Kimber*, thirty-two, white. Flip's girlfriend. Kimber is an intelligent woman with a quick wit and a sincere warmth. Unlike Taylor, her social status matches that of the LeVays, with, of course, the undeniable privilege of whiteness. Of this she is aware and, on some level, appalled.

# ACT 1

## PROLOGUE

[TAYLOR *stands at lip of stage in a tight spot. She wears a stunningly tailored black suit, heels, and dark sunglasses. She fingers a funeral program.* KENT, *a young man in a slightly rumpled but good dark suit walks past, exits, and enters again. They stare at each other; she refuses to speak first.*]

KENT: I know you.

TAYLOR: Really? At a funeral?

KENT: No. No. I think I know you.

TAYLOR: And again I say . . . At a funeral?

KENT: Are you a cultural anthropologist?

TAYLOR: Absolutely not. Not even for fun.

KENT: You go to the university?

TAYLOR: No.

KENT: Were you at Harvard in ninety-seven?

TAYLOR: Aw jeez.

KENT: What?

TAYLOR: I thought you were picking me up.

KENT: No. At a funeral?

TAYLOR: You were just, recognizing me?

KENT: Yeah, 'cause, like I said, I think I know you.

[Pause.]

You know where? Dr. Bradley Scott was guest lecturing a couple of years ago. Social stratification among the black elite.

TAYLOR: Yep. The Hilton Head Howards versus the Vineyard LeVays. He's always had a sort of sycophantic relationship to the well heeled.

[Beat.]

Actually, I wasn't there for the lecture. I just needed to see Dr. Bradley Scott.

KENT: You knew him well?

TAYLOR: You could say that.

KENT: Is it a sordid tale?

TAYLOR: You could say that.

KENT: I'm sorry for your loss.

TAYLOR: Thank you. You knew him well?

KENT: No, no. I'm almost embarrassed to be here. I'm a fan. I think he was a genius.

[*Beat.*]

    Were you avoiding his wife?

TAYLOR: Yes.

KENT: When did you meet him?

TAYLOR: Twenty-seven years ago.

KENT: I'm sorry?

TAYLOR: Me too.

[*Pause.*]

KENT: Kent. Kent LeVay.

TAYLOR: Of the Vineyard LeVays? Oh. I see.

KENT: Yeah. And you?

TAYLOR: Taylor Bradley Scott.

KENT: Oh.

TAYLOR: Of the dead Dr. James Bradley Scott, Bradley Scotts.

[*Beat.*]

KENT: Oh.

TAYLOR: Yeah.

[TAYLOR *begins to sob.*]

    Damn. I'm out of Kleenex.

[KENT *hands her a handkerchief.*]

KENT: I'm sorry. Here . . . God, I'm so sorry, and here I was going on about how I met you, and your dad and stuff . . .

TAYLOR: It's OK.

KENT: It was rude.

TAYLOR: No really, it's OK.

KENT: So he's your dad?

TAYLOR: Was.

KENT: Oh, yeah right. Sorry.

TAYLOR: Sort of was. It's complicated.

KENT: Like your stepdad or something.

TAYLOR: No . . . our relationship was decidedly biological. I'm sorry, I didn't expect to be this upset. It sort of sneaks up on you.

KENT: Seems like you should be upset.

TAYLOR: Maybe. But I barely knew him.

[*Beat.* TAYLOR *blows her nose.*]

So you hang out at funerals of people you don't know often?

KENT: He did write a book about my family.

TAYLOR: That's stretching it . . .

KENT: Well, we made the title. I like his politics. He's not afraid of the truth, doesn't care about upsetting black folks or white folks, and I admire that. I'd like to be like that. I like to think I am like that.

TAYLOR: So you're an academic, in pursuit of mainstream fame.

KENT: No. Well, I'm, I've been a student for a long time, but pretty much in pursuit of nothing, specific.

TAYLOR: It's a little strange that you carry a handkerchief. It seems not quite of this century.

KENT: One of my mother's rules that stuck. She isn't quite of this century.

[*Awkward silence.*]

TAYLOR: Can I show you something?

[TAYLOR *opens the funeral program and points out a sentence for* KENT.]

Read this . . .

KENT: Dr. James Bradley Scott, born—

TAYLOR: No, here—

KENT: —survived by wife, Gabrielle, and two children, Martin and—

TAYLOR: —This.

[*She puts her finger exactly where she needs him to read.*]

KENT: —and one child from a previous marriage.

TAYLOR: That's me.

KENT: Wow.

[*Pause.*]

Listen, for what it's worth. I've lived with my dad my whole life and barely know him.

TAYLOR: Was that supposed to comfort me?

KENT: Maybe. Did it?

TAYLOR: Not what you said. The gesture maybe. OK.

KENT: Well, you take care, OK?

TAYLOR: You're nice.

[*Blackout.*]

# SCENE 1

[*Curtains rise to reveal the bisected front half of a two-story Martha's Vineyard cottage. The decor is tasteful, casual, comfortable, and extraordinarily expensive in its utter lack of pretension. The house defines comfort—smooth, well-worn leathers; cashmere throws; rustic aged wood; books, books, books, and more books. The living room is dark, shutters closed; fabric covers the furniture. The kitchen curtains are open, lights on. A purse and jacket are draped over a chair. An impressive pile of boxes and shopping bags of groceries takes up a quarter of the counter space and floor beneath it. Someone has begun putting away groceries and abandoned the job. CHERYL enters from upstairs, listening to an iPod. She's the picture of youth and resentful efficiency. She opens curtains whenever she passes a window. Occasionally she cannot help but dance to the jam blasting in her ears. She carries a large wicker basket into which she throws the sheets covering the furniture as she removes them. CHERYL exits into the house with the basket. Offstage a car pulls into a gravel driveway. Car doors open and close. Through the windows we see and hear KENT, weighed down with expensive, aesthetically subdued luggage, followed by TAYLOR in cutoff jeans, faded T-shirt, and bandanna. She carries a large, well-worn duffle bag. They laugh and talk all the way to the door.*]

TAYLOR: Is there anyone in there?

KENT: Probably. Oh shit, I forgot my computer. Go on in.

TAYLOR: Shouldn't we knock?

KENT: No honey, we belong here . . .

[*Through the windows the audience sees* KENT, *running to the car.* TAYLOR *opens the door and steps over the luggage and into the house.*]

TAYLOR [*taking it all in*]: Wow.

[*Beat.*]

   Holy . . . Wow.

[KENT *enters.*]

   This is all yours?

KENT: My family's . . .

TAYLOR: All that, all this, around the drive, and that little house?

KENT: That's the guesthouse.

TAYLOR: Wow. OK. Well, I was gonna marry you for love. But now maybe I'll have to marry you for money.

KENT: I thought you said yes so we could sleep together at family reunions.

TAYLOR: Only my mother is so provincial.

KENT: Honey Bee, that's not provincial, that's black.

[TAYLOR *explores the room for a moment. She checks out the family pictures in small frames on the tables.*]

TAYLOR [*pointing to a painting*]: Spoon. Spoon honey . . . Is this a real Romare—

KENT: Bearden. Yes.

TAYLOR: And that's a real—

KENT: Um.

TAYLOR: And . . . this one . . .

KENT: Yes.

TAYLOR: Oh my God.

KENT: Mom's classy. French, Italian, Swahili. Undergrad art history, master's child development, MFA interdisciplinary arts integration, all so she could be here with warm cookies when we got home from school.

TAYLOR: Should I be intimidated?

KENT: Absolutely.

[TAYLOR *approaches an impressive display of butterflies and beetles mounted in a framed glass case.*]

TAYLOR: You didn't tell me. Someone's a collector?

KENT: What?

TAYLOR: The butterflies . . .

KENT: Aesthetic. Mom's only relationship with bugs is through the exterminator. She has him on speed dial. Called him once because there were too many ants . . . outside.

TAYLOR [*crossing over to the family pictures*]: Oh . . . these are amazing. Wow. Look how beautiful the clothes are . . . and the people. Who is this . . . ?

KENT: Grandma LeVay, Dad's mom, we lost her ten years ago . . . Oh . . . And this is Great-Great-Grandfather Whitcomb. The Great Sea Captain.

TAYLOR: He's so handsome.

KENT: Yeah, I got his good looks.

TAYLOR: I've seen this picture before . . .

KENT: Yeah, in your Dad's book . . .

TAYLOR: Of course . . .

KENT: He was never a slave . . . He was a shipper.

TAYLOR: Of what . . .

KENT: We don't talk about that. Anyway he saved the mayor's son from a boating accident. As a reward the mayor gave him this land on which he built this house, making the Whitcombs the first blacks to own land anywhere on the Vineyard.

TAYLOR: Wow. It's beautiful.

[*Beat.*]

I'm nervous. Now I'm really nervous.

KENT: Why?

TAYLOR: I'm supposed to be. You're bringing home your fiancée.

[KENT *walks to her and pulls her into a comfortable embrace.*]

KENT: You're adorable. They'll love you. Let me show you around before you unpack your nets and jars.

[KENT *picks her up and throws her onto the sofa.*]

This, my love, is the family sofa.

[*A playful embrace turns into a genuine moment of groping and passion.* KENT *unzips* TAYLOR's *pants. She slowly but firmly moves away.* KENT *won't be discouraged.*]

You know Ma's gonna have us in separate rooms.

TAYLOR: That's so black of her.

KENT: Honey Bee, give me a little sugar.

[*She does. The kiss gets dangerous.*]

TAYLOR: OK, OK. I'm not having your mom walk in on me with my ass up in the air like some kind of bad urban legend or something.

KENT: Fine, I'll feed my other carnal needs.

[KENT *makes his way to the kitchen.*]

I wonder if Ms. Ellie left food.

[KENT *kisses* TAYLOR *on the cheek and bounds through the swinging door to the kitchen. Surveying the groceries, he searches through the bags, finds cookies, and munches while he begins to put away the provisions. In the living room,* TAYLOR *zips her pants and begins moving suitcases to the bottom of the staircase.* CHERYL *enters from upper stage right, dragging the basket now overflowing with sheets.* TAYLOR *is startled.*]

TAYLOR: Oh . . . Oh.

CHERYL: Sorry.

TAYLOR: You startled me.

CHERYL [*struggling with the basket across the room and backing through the swinging kitchen door*]: Oh God. Hi . . . Uhgghhh . . .

I'm not ready. I thought Flip said evening. This is afternoon. Where is he? Kent!

[*In the kitchen* KENT *helps her set down the basket and embraces her.*]

KENT: Look at you! You're all grown up! You start college yet?

CHERYL: Uh-uh. Oh, oh . . . so that must be your woman out there? She cute.

KENT: I think so.

CHERYL: I'm so behind. You caught the first ferry? Mama makes it look easy.

[CHERYL *begins putting away the remainder of the groceries.*]

Hopefully I start school next winter. Mama's sick, so you gotta settle for me.

[*Beat.*]

But that's aw'ight 'cause I always did like coming up here.

[KENT *helps* CHERYL *put away groceries. It's clear they've done this to-gether before.*]

Depending on how Mama's doing I might be able to fit in a class or two in the fall . . .

[KENT *and* CHERYL *continue to put away groceries, while in the living room* TAYLOR *crosses to the doorway to pick up suitcases.* FLIP *enters through the front door.*]

FLIP: Oh, hi . . .

[TAYLOR *turns around. Both are shocked.*]

TAYLOR: Harold?

FLIP: Flip. Please.

[*Scene switches to the kitchen.*]

KENT: . . . You know where? . . .

CHERYL: I'm still waiting to hear. I applied everywhere . . . I wanna stay near Mama though, maybe NYU, Columbia . . . Princeton's kinda far . . .

[*Scene switches to the living room.*]

TAYLOT: Flip.

[*Beat.*]

He's talked about you. But I didn't put it together.

FLIP: Yeah, I heard about you, also . . . it didn't even occur to me.

TAYLOR: Taylor . . .

FLIP: I know.

[*Scene switches to the kitchen.*]

KENT: You'll probably have your pick . . .

CHERYL: Well, I don't like to brag . . .

[*Scene switches to the living room.*]

TAYLOR: Yeah. OK.

FLIP: All right then.

| | |
|---|---|
| TAYLOR: | FLIP: |
| Well, it's good to see you. | What you been up to? |

[TAYLOR *moves in for a hug,* FLIP *a shake. They fumble and eventually settle on an awkward half embrace. Scene switches to the kitchen.*]

CHERYL: You staying long?

KENT: Few weeks, if Ma and Taylor hit it off.

CHERYL: She seems nice. It'll be OK.

[*Scene switches to the living room.*]

FLIP: So, where's my bro?

TAYLOR: He's in the kitchen with . . . ?

[*Scene switches to the kitchen.*]

CHERYL: Oh . . . you can hand me that . . .

[*Scene switches to the living room.*]

FLIP: Ms. Ellie?

TAYLOR: I don't know?

FLIP: Large, pleasant, older black lady?

TAYLOR: No, no. Pretty, young. Nice. She was already here.

FLIP: Kimber beat me?

TAYLOR: Spoon said you were in Aspen.

FLIP: Spoon?

TAYLOR: Kent. I'm sorry, pet name. Yeah, I thought you two were coming up later.

FLIP: I cut it short.

[*A burst of laughter comes from the kitchen, where* KENT *juggles and then tosses* CHERYL *corn, which she deposits in the fridge.*]

I had to fly back for an emergency. Kimber got here too early. I wanted time to smooth the way, you know.

[*Beat.*]

TAYLOR: No.

[*Beat.*]

She said we got here too early.

FLIP [*heading toward the kitchen*]: She did, did she?

[TAYLOR *follows* FLIP. FLIP *enters the kitchen.*]

Honey, you weren't supposed to come for another . . .

KENT: Honey?

CHERYL: Hey!

FLIP: Cheryl! Look at you, all grown up.

[FLIP *hugs* CHERYL. *The audience sees that* CHERYL *carries an intense and painful crush on* FLIP.]

CHERYL: Yeah, well, you know I'll be going to college. Gonna load up the science on the front end so I can go premed.

[*Awkward beat.*]

Like you were when you went, to college.

FLIP: A long time ago. [*Hugging* KENT] Hey man, met your girl. You coulda done worse.

[*Beat.* FLIP *looks around expectantly.*]

So what did you do with her?

KENT: What?

[TAYLOR *enters the kitchen.*]

FLIP: Your girl said my girl was in the kitchen.

TAYLOR: Oh, I thought she was . . . I'm confused.

FLIP: Naw . . . my girl's still where I left her. I have a little ground laying to do with the folks first.

TAYLOR [*to* CHERYL]: Then you are?

CHERYL: Oh, Cheryl. I'm working for the LeVays.

KENT: Cheryl's mom, Ms. Ellie, has helped Mom for years . . . but now she's all grown up.

CHERYL [*grinning at* FLIP]: I am.

TAYLOR: Oh . . . you're the maid.

[*Awkward silence.* CHERYL *runs water in the sink and deposits several live lobsters.* TAYLOR *helps put the remaining food away.*]

[*To* CHERYL] Where do the grits go?

CHERYL: We keep the dry goods in the fridge . . . it's so humid here, things get kind of—

TAYLOR [*to* KENT]: What did he mean, ground laying?

KENT: Yeah, Flip's girl is a little melanin challenged.

CHERYL: Melanin challenged?

KENT: She's, of the other persuasion . . .

TAYLOR: Not in the tribe, huh?

FLIP: She's cool. Studies race dynamics in inner-city schools.

TAYLOR: As opposed to the outer city?

CHERYL [*just getting it*]: Oh, she white?

KENT AND FLIP: She's Italian.

KENT: So, this is Taylor.

FLIP: Yeah . . . we go way back.

[FLIP *and* TAYLOR *exchange a look, which* CHERYL *catches.*]

KENT: Yeah?

TAYLOR: No.

FLIP: Yeah, all the way back to the living room.

TAYLOR: It's nice to . . . meet you.

[*They shake hands.* FLIP'S *phone rings.*]

FLIP: Hold on . . .

[FLIP *looks at caller ID.*]

I don't answer it on vacation.

CHERYL: What about your patients?

[FLIP *pushes a couple of buttons on his new, sexy, status phone and starts to put the phone in his pocket.*]

KENT: Ohhh . . . nice. You got one . . .

FLIP: Oh yeah . . . My assistant stood in line for twelve hours.

KENT: Sweet . . . Sexy . . .

FLIP: Damn straight . . .

CHERYL [*to* TAYLOR, *who is holding a big box of oatmeal*]: Oh, you can leave the oatmeal on the counter, we go through it pretty fast. [*To* FLIP] Flip, you never liked white girls.

FLIP: She's Italian.

KENT [*to* CHERYL]: Where are Mom and Dad? I thought they were supposed to be here—

CHERYL [*to* FLIP]: Dr. LeVay got called into an emergency . . . They should be here early tomorrow. You want me to make dinner?

KENT: Naw, thanks, I think I'll show Taylor around . . . You wanna come, Flip?

FLIP: I'm cool. I'll stay here and help our girl with the house.

[KENT *and* TAYLOR *exit kitchen while* CHERYL *and* FLIP *continue with kitchen chores.*]

KENT: So, what's first?

TAYLOR: I don't know . . . whatever you wanna do. You could show me the ocean.

KENT: You've seen oceans. We could go down to the wharf . . .

TAYLOR: The wharf?

KENT: Town. Look around, lots of shops and galleries . . .

TAYLOR: I've seen towns.

KENT: Maybe I should show you my room.

TAYLOR: I've seen rooms.

KENT: Maybe there's something in my room you've seen before that you'd like to see again?

TAYLOR: Flip's girlfriend is white?

KENT [*laughing*]: No. She's Italian.

TAYLOR: Will your folks disapprove?

KENT: Naw, that's what I'm here for.

TAYLOR: That doesn't bode well for me.

KENT: No, it's not like that . . . They'll love you. Dad'll think you're too good for me.

TAYLOR: Well, I am.

[*Beat.*]

You brought the hard copy of your manuscript, right?

KENT: Yeah.

TAYLOR: You'll show it to them?

KENT: If I feel like it.

TAYLOR: What does that mean?

KENT: It means, if I feel like it . . .

[*Lights fade as they make their way upstairs.*]

# SCENE 2

[*Late evening, same day.* FLIP, KENT, *and* TAYLOR *lounge in the living room. They're playing Trivial Pursuit.* CHERYL *clears take-out Chinese from the coffee table, moving in and out of the kitchen.*]

FLIP: —and this little blonde salesgirl, she's just on me. So I say, look, I've traveled all over the world, I'm a doctor dammit, why you wanna sweat me like that—

TAYLOR: Stop talking, maybe he'll take his turn.

FLIP: I'm just saying. What the hell am I going to steal from Pottery Barn, like—

CHERYL: You could put a candle in your pocket or something.

FLIP: That was rhetorical, Cheryl. [*To* KENT] Go.

KENT: What's green?

TAYLOR: You know that.

FLIP: You're sure you won't play, Cheryl?

CHERYL: I'm saying, they shouldn't follow you around because you're a person.

FLIP: What?

CHERYL: You shouldn't be harassed because you're human.

KENT [*to* FLIP]: What's green?

FLIP [*to* KENT]: Come on . . . [*To* CHERYL] Like I said, not just a person, a well-dressed, well-read, well-traveled person.

KENT: So remind me. What's green?

TAYLOR: You know that.

CHERYL: So they should follow around a guy who works for, say, the phone company, just not you? [*Exiting to the kitchen*] Green is science and nature.

TAYLOR: Cheryl's right. That's classist. Now play.

FLIP: Why are we doing this?

KENT AND TAYLOR: Quality family time.

FLIP: Oh please. [*Yelling toward the kitchen*] Stop working and come on and play, Cheryl . . . You'll be busy enough when Mom and Dad get here.

TAYLOR [*Yelling toward the kitchen*]: You can take my place and I'll finish up the dishes.

CHERYL [*poking head through door*]: I hate that game. Besides, if your folks came and I was . . .

TAYLOR: Really, I don't mind.

[TAYLOR *begins clearing the dishes.* CHERYL *takes them from her.*]

CHERYL: It's fine. Really. It's my job.

[CHERYL *exits to kitchen.*]

TAYLOR: I was just trying to help.

FLIP: Now who's holding things up? Play, so we can finish the damn game.

TAYLOR: I like the game. You would too if you were invested in winning.

FLIP: Yeah, bro, where's your fighting spirit?

KENT: It's trivia . . . Trivial Pursuit. The pursuit of things trivial. Implicit in the name is the reason for my lack of investment.

FLIP: That's not implicit, that's intrinsic . . . intrinsic to the name . . .

TAYLOR: Inherent.

FLIP AND KENT: No.

TAYLOR: It's entertainment.

KENT: Jesus, fine. Green, for a piece of pie.

TAYLOR: What Russian physiologist went to the dogs to write *Conditioned Reflexes*? You always get the easy ones.

KENT: Pavlov.

TAYLOR: I need a first name.

KENT: That's ridiculous.

TAYLOR: No, it's the rules.

FLIP: She's right.

KENT: I don't want to play.

TAYLOR: Oh my God. You suck.

[CHERYL *enters with a pitcher of lemonade and glasses.*]

CHERYL: Ivan. Ivan Pavlov.

[*Beat.*]

What? I can't know that?

KENT: So here, you win the pie.

CHERYL [*to* FLIP]: Here Flip, you can have it.

KENT: Come on Cheryl, have a little fun . . .

[KENT *follows* CHERYL *toward the kitchen with lemonade.*]

CHERYL [*exiting to the kitchen with* KENT]: I can't play with you guys like that this summer. Mom isn't here; I have work to do.

TAYLOR: Fine. [*To* FLIP] Your turn.

CHERYL [*to* KENT, *as* FLIP *rolls*]: She's a little serious about this, isn't she?

TAYLOR: Hurry up, honey! You're missing my brilliance. History . . . OK. What South Vietnamese president was assassinated by his generals in 1963?

FLIP: Let me read that.

TAYLOR: Can he do that?

[KENT *has entered from the kitchen.*]

FLIP: I get South Vietnamese president; he gets Pavlov.

DAD [*entering from study*]: Ngo Dinh Diem.

KENT: Dad!

DAD: Yes, sir. The South Vietnamese president. I met him in fifty-nine.

FLIP: You made it.

DAD: Sons. You know, a little-known thing about Ngo Dinh—

KENT: We didn't hear you drive up . . .

DAD: Oh, I flew in, had the shuttle drop me off at the end of the drive.

FLIP: You didn't bring the car?

DAD: Your mom's bringing it tomorrow . . .

FLIP: Tomorrow? I don't understand?

DAD: So, little known fact about Ngo Dinh . . .

TAYLOR: Dr. LeVay . . . So nice to meet you . . . I'm . . .

DAD: I'm sorry . . . going on like that. [*To* FLIP, *assuming* TAYLOR *is his guest*] Flip, you weren't going to introduce us?

KENT: No. Dad, this is Taylor. Taylor Bradley Scott. Beautiful, isn't she . . . ?

TAYLOR [*to* KENT]: You didn't tell them about me?

DAD: Oh. [*Momentarily confused, as he's assumed* TAYLOR'*s with* FLIP] . . . OK. [*Assessing her*] Nice. [*To* KENT] Well done. Ms. Bradley Scott . . .

[DAD *has recovered.*]

Beautiful doesn't do this exceptional creature justice. It's an honor my dear.

KENT: Dad . . . I mentioned Taylor . . . my fiancée . . . Her father was—

[DAD *kisses her hand and bows with a flourish.* KENT *and* FLIP *exchange a knowing look: he's always had a way with the ladies.*]

DAD: Of course . . . James Bradley Scott . . . yes, of course . . . Well, again, so nice to meet you . . .

TAYLOR: Dr. LeVay.

DAD: Too formal.

[*Beat.*]

"Dad" would be weird, huh? How 'bout you call me Joseph?

TAYLOR: OK, Doctor.

[*Beat.*]

Sir . . . uh, Joseph.

DAD: Your dad was a great man. Great man. I just regret I didn't have the opportunity to know him.

TAYLOR: Yeah. Yeah, I regret that too.

DAD: It's been a year now? So sorry for your loss. Grief's a bitch, huh?

TAYLOR: Guess so.

DAD: Which was my favorite, you boys remember, I made you read it and write a report one summer. [*Searching on shelf for book*] Oh yeah, um, it's right there, right there . . . oh yeah, *The Bonds of Intellectual Freedom.*

TAYLOR: That's a lot of people's favorite. [*To* FLIP *and* KENT] Are we playing or not guys?

DAD: Won him a Pulitzer, didn't it?

TAYLOR: His second. So, whose turn?

DAD: Kickin' their asses, I see.

TAYLOR: Yes sir. But it's no fun, they don't want to play.

DAD: Because you're kickin' their asses.

TAYLOR: I'm trying.

[CHERYL *enters, drying her hands on a dish towel.*]

DAD: Cheryl! As I live and breathe. This is not the little girl I saw last year, surely not. Boys, there's a ravishing young woman toiling away in our kitchen.

CHERYL: Hi, Dr. LeVay. Mom said you'd know. Wasn't Mrs. LeVay supposed to tell you? Mom's sick. So I'm here. I came up Thursday. Where is Mrs. LeVay?

DAD [*hugging* CHERYL]: I'm sorry to hear that; please give her my best. No, Michelle must have forgotten to pass this little tidbit on. I'm sure we're in good hands.

CHERYL: Can I fix you something?

DAD: That'd be great. You know what I like.

CHERYL: On black or white rye?

DAD: Let's keep it black. Extra mustard, OK.

CHERYL: I know.

[CHERYL *exits to kitchen.*]

FLIP: So . . . where's Ma?

DAD: Your mom and I would have driven up tomorrow, but she thought she might have morning meetings—

FLIP: So she told you to just go ahead?

KENT: You just left? You couldn't wait for her? . . .

FLIP [*trying to save* KENT *from himself*]: Hey, hey, hey . . .

DAD [*to* KENT]: What?

TAYLOR: Dr. LeVay, the house is beautiful.

DAD [*to* KENT]: So, what's up with you? Found a career you want to stick with for five minutes?

KENT: Flip has a friend joining him. You should ask him about her . . .

DAD: So, you're going to support your beautiful wife writing books now, I hear.

TAYLOR: Spoon is very talented. And I'm supporting myself just fine. You really should read his—

DAD: Spoon?

TAYLOR: Oh, my nickname for him. He brought the manuscript—

KENT: Taylor, don't . . .

DAD: That's sweet, flatware. So son, you're a very talented fiction writer for whom I paid to get a law degree, a business degree, and a master's in sociology.

TAYLOR: Spoon just got a publisher.

DAD: Random House? Dell?

KENT: It's a small, reputable house . . .

DAD: Oh. Small . . .

KENT: Reputable . . .

TAYLOR: Maybe Spoo— Kent told you? I'm doing a postdoc at Johns Hopkins. Entomology.

FLIP: Dad. You've only been here ten minutes, lighten up. I read the novel, it's good. Come on, let's get you some food.

[FLIP *and* DAD *exit to the kitchen, where* CHERYL *has set the table and is preparing an elaborate sandwich.*]

CHERYL: Oh . . . Flip. Can I make you one too?

FLIP: No thanks. I'm cool. Gotta watch my girlish figure.

CHERYL: You're funny.

[*Action continues in the kitchen as the focus shifts to the living room.*]

TAYLOR: That was intense.

KENT: Not even. That was mild.

TAYLOR: You're shrinking.

KENT: I'm fine.

[*Scene switches to the kitchen.*]

DAD: Pickles.

CHERYL: Yes sir, I know.

[*Scene switches to the living room.*]

TAYLOR: Please don't let him turn you into a thirteen-year-old. I like you grown up.

KENT: That's what parents do.

TAYLOR: Parents who are around I guess.

[*Scene switches to the kitchen.*]

DAD: The beef is shaved.

DAD AND CHERYL: Not sliced—

CHERYL: Right.

[*Scene switches to the living room.*]

TAYLOR: You didn't tell them about me?

KENT: It's not that deep. Really. I told Ma. She probably decided to let Dad meet you . . . He's hard on me . . . It would have been a thing. More of what you just saw, you know.

TAYLOR [*cuddling on sofa*]: So, you wanna keep playing? I'm just a piece of pie away from victory.

KENT: No . . . No, please don't make me play . . .

[TAYLOR *kisses* KENT.]

TAYLOR: You're a good man, Kent LeVay. And you're a fine writer. The world will know it.

KENT: Let's go upstairs. You can remind me how grown up I am.

TAYLOR [*as they are crossing over to the stairs*]: Well how grown up you wanna be?

KENT: How grown up you wanna make me feel?

[*They exit upstairs. Scene switches to the kitchen.*]

DAD: So, you have a guest coming, huh? An important one?

FLIP: A friend, Dad.

[CHERYL *moves closer, unnoticed.*]

DAD: You don't usually bring your friends around when we're all here.

FLIP: She's cool. Met her at the practice. Came in yelling at me about her mother's lift. Said I was taking advantage. She was right.

DAD: Met your mom under similar circumstances.

CHERYL: Well, if that'll be all?

DAD: Have you heard this story, Cheryl?

CHERYL: Every anniversary, every birthday, every Thanksgiving. So, I'll just be in the . . .

[CHERYL *escapes to the living room and begins straightening up. Through the scene she moves between living room and kitchen, deposit-*

*ing dirty dishes, fluffing pillows, and so on. She is seldom, if ever, acknowledged.*]

FLIP: We've all heard this story, Dad—

DAD: One of those brown-bag cotillions.

FLIP: Yeah, you've told us—

DAD: You know, they'd hold the bag up to your face—

FLIP: Many times—

DAD: —run the comb through your hair and if the comb can't get through, or the bag's lighter than you, well—

DAD AND FLIP: clearly you're at the wrong party.

[CHERYL *deposits beer bottles into the recycling bin, scrapes plates, and stacks them in the sink.*]

DAD: So I fail on both sides, and I'll never forget, this—

DAD AND FLIP: yellow-waisted girl in an ugly-ass bright pink dress—

DAD: —is saying, I'm sorry Dr. LeVay, but uh, I'm not allowed, you understand . . . And just then, this beautiful woman—

FLIP: in a blue dress with long brown curls and gray eyes—

DAD: Let me tell the story! This beautiful woman walks in. [*Referring to sandwich*] Cheryl. That looks delicious. [*To* FLIP] And she says, Dr. LeVay, I read about you in last month's *Harvard Review,* and I cannot believe you're going to just stand there and let this bitch turn you away, I would have danced with you . . . and she went on and on.

[DAD *pauses dramatically.*]

FLIP: Fine.

[*Beat.*]

Did you get in?

DAD: Hell no. But I got your mother's name and number.

DAD AND FLIP: And the rest is history.

FLIP: So, my friend is Italian.

[CHERYL *exits into the living room. During the following, she does a little straightening, finally leaving the unfinished business for morning. She notices James Bradley Scott's novel on the coffee table, reads the jacket description, flips through it, places it on a side table, and exits upstairs.*]

DAD: You mean, she's white.

FLIP: She's Italian.

DAD: Oh, well. She here?

FLIP: She's coming tomorrow.

DAD [*amused*]: Wanted to lay the groundwork with your mom, huh?

FLIP: Well, with both of you. I just thought it would be good if you knew.

DAD: You sound like you're embarrassed.

FLIP: No, just, aware. Mom's gonna freak isn't she.

DAD: Hard to say . . . She's got some other stuff on her mind.

FLIP: She alright?

DAD: Yeah, you know women. You been to visit this girl's people?

FLIP: Only the artist aunt in the city. We'll drive over in a few weeks. They're in Kenny.

DAD: Bunkport? Oh. OK. I'm sure they'll be happy to see you.

FLIP: Seriously, Dad, what's up with Mom?

DAD: Why you ask?

FLIP: Just not like her to get here after us. She lives for this.

DAD: I told you, she has meetings.

FLIP: Yeah, OK.

[FLIP *gets up to leave.*]

   Hey Dad, take it easy on Kent, all right.

DAD: I don't know what you're talking about.

FLIP: Sure you do.

[KENT *has entered with his manuscript, unnoticed.*]

DAD: The boy's a fuckup. Hey . . . I don't set unreasonably high standards. But I've given you boys everything. There's no need for floundering.

KENT: Just came down for some milk. Seems if we can't all live up to the high standards you set, at least we can watch our calcium intake.

FLIP: That's what I'm talking about Dad. It's harsh.

KENT: I don't need you to defend me.

FLIP: You don't. That's funny. OK. Then I'm out.

[FLIP *exits.*]

KENT [*pulling manuscript out of his back pocket*]: I've been wanting to talk with you about something.

DAD: What, you're starting dental school next fall?

KENT: No. I just thought I could show you . . .

DAD: Look, son. Flip's right, that was harsh, I'm sorry. But I swear I don't know what to do with you.

KENT: Do with me?

DAD: It's time to step up. You're about to have a wife, God help you. Maybe start a family? You can't be out there like you've been, trying to find yourself and what not. It's not about you anymore. [*Pulling out his Blackberry*] I'll help you. [*Scrolling through his address book*] Figure out what you want to do with your life and get back to me . . . I'll make some calls. But I'm not entertaining this mess about now I'm a writer . . . Damn boy . . . man up. Get a job.

[*Beat.*]

You have something to say?

KENT [*hiding his manuscript*]: No, sir.

DAD: I didn't think so.

[*Lights fade.*]

## SCENE 3

[*Later, same evening.* CHERYL *is speaking quietly on the phone.*]

CHERYL: . . . I don't make waffles. Ma . . . Ma! It's not efficient. There's a kitchen full of food . . . I used your list . . . yeah. But I got some other stuff. I hear you, but—

[*Beat.*]

But—

[*Beat.*]

Uh-huh. Yes, ma'am. Listen, Ma . . . there's like a b'jillion kinds of cereal, granola, yogurt, whole milk, two percent, soy, heavy cream, raspberries, strawberries, bagels, lox . . .

[DAD *enters and begins rummaging through cabinets in kitchen.*]

OK. Ma, I've gotta go. Yeah, yes, ma'am, but really, I have to go . . . uh-huh.

[*Long pause.*]

Ask, "If there's anything he wants to say . . ." OK, I'll ask, but I don't understand. OK. Love you too. Feel better all right. Bye. [*To* DAD] Sorry about that.

DAD: Oh, no problem . . . I was just—

CHERYL: Looking for something to eat?

DAD: Right.

CHERYL: What do you have a taste for? I could whip something up.

DAD: Not sure . . .

CHERYL: Sandwich?

DAD: Maybe . . .

CHERYL: Soup?

DAD: I don't know . . .

CHERYL: Maybe there's something specific you were looking for?

DAD: Like what?

CHERYL: I don't know. Maybe something you were saving for a special occasion?

DAD: Like?

CHERYL: Caviar?

DAD: Have you ever known me to eat anything raw, Ellie?

CHERYL: Cheryl.

DAD: Of course.

CHERYL: I think what you're looking for is behind the flour bin.

DAD: You think, huh?

CHERYL: I thought it was Mom's.

DAD: Behind the flour bin, you say?

CHERYL: Yes, sir.

DAD: Then I guess you know what else I need.

[CHERYL *points to a cabinet near the refrigerator.* DAD *pulls out hot sauce.* CHERYL *reaches behind the flour bin and pulls out a large jar of pickled pigs' feet.*]

Pickled pigs' feet.

CHERYL: Can I get you a bowl?

DAD: No, I'm good now. Thank you, dear.

[CHERYL *begins to shuck corn.*]

Would you like to join me?

CHERYL: Oh God no!

[*Beat.*]

Thank you, sir.

DAD: That's funny. Too good for the finer things, huh?

CHERYL: No, it's just . . .

DAD: Your mother likes them cold, you know.

CHERYL: Yes, sir. I've had them before. When I was too young to know better.

DAD: Yeah, my kids won't touch them either. That's why I have to hide them. Or I'll never hear the end of it.

[CHERYL *brushes silk from corn.* DAD *eats. Pause.*]

So how is Ellie?

CHERYL: Well, she pretty sick.

DAD: You told me. With what?

CHERYL: Either they don't know or she won't tell me. But it must be bad . . . You know she never misses a day of work . . .

DAD: Nice of you to fill in.

CHERYL: Oh, of course.

DAD: You talk to Mrs. LeVay?

CHERYL: This morning. But that was Mom on the phone just now.

DAD: What'd she have to say?

CHERYL: Mom?

DAD: Mrs. LeVay.

CHERYL: She said I shouldn't let you eat cheese . . . reminded me to make sure Juan turns over the compost . . . Flip's allergic to nuts, but I knew that . . .

DAD: Just, if you needed to talk about anything.

CHERYL: OK. Sure.

[*Beat.*]

I'm struggling with which school would be best for science . . . or if I should do a liberal arts thing my first year . . .

DAD: Just if you needed to . . .

CHERYL: Right. Of course. I'm sorry. Yes. No, it's good. Well, Mom did tell me to ask you if, if, . . . um—

[TAYLOR *enters in pajamas and a robe.*]

TAYLOR: Dr. LeVay.

DAD: Joseph.

TAYLOR: Right. Hi, Cheryl. Um, Spoon asked me to grab him some milk, I was just . . .

CHERYL: I'll get it.

[CHERYL *starts to get glasses down.*]

TAYLOR: Oh, just tell me where things are. I'm perfectly capable.

CHERYL: Didn't think you weren't "capable," just thought you wanted some milk. Fine, glasses up there. Milk in the fridge.

[TAYLOR *takes down two glasses and pours milk while* DAD *and* CHERYL *continue to talk.*]

DAD: So, about the house . . .

CHERYL: OK, Mrs. LeVay asked me to make her a list of repairs for contractors.

[*She walks over to a list on the fridge.*]

So far I have gutters, the light fixture in the upstairs bathroom, some loose latticework under the porch. Oh, and the storm windows and shutters.

DAD: I could have the boys do that.

CHERYL: OK. Should I cross it off?

DAD: Leave it on.

CHERYL: OK then.

DAD: Great.

[CHERYL *has finished shucking and rinses off the corn and puts it in the fridge while* DAD *eats.*]

CHERYL: So yeah, Mom said to ask you . . . I don't know, like, if there's something you want to say to me . . .

DAD: No, dear.

CHERYL: I don't know . . . I didn't quite understand . . . something you might want to say . . .

DAD: No.

CHERYL: OK . . . but Mama said . . .

DAD: I said no. Don't you have something to do?

[CHERYL *exits to the living room. After a moment of idle dusting,* CHERYL *sees Dr. Bradley Scott's book, curls up on a chair, and reads in the glow of a lamp.*]

TAYLOR: Milk?

DAD: What? No. Thank you.

TAYLOR: Gets a little cool here at night, huh?

DAD: Yes. Yes it is. A little cool.

[KENT *enters the kitchen.*]

KENT: Baby, what's taking you . . . Oh, Dad. Found the pigs' feet I see. [*To* TAYLOR] You've been down here forever; bed's getting cold.

DAD: Taylor's still trying to ingratiate herself . . . That takes a little time.

[DAD *screws the lid on the jar of pigs' feet and takes them with him.*]

Well I'm off. See you kids later.

[DAD *exits.*]

TAYLOR: What's up with your dad and Cheryl?

KENT: What?

TAYLOR: I don't know, they just did the weirdest dance . . .

KENT: Dancing?

TAYLOR: Noooo . . . Just weird, I don't know.

KENT: You haven't figured out yet that my family's weird? Wait till Mom gets here, they'll snap back in line. Can I read a rewrite?

[KENT *pulls some pages from his back pocket, and they settle in at the table. In the living room,* CHERYL *continues reading in her small pool of light. She is thoroughly engrossed.*]

See, I wanted the confrontation with Michael and his dad to be subtle . . . It can't be histrionic, or it's cheap . . . OK . . . here it is . . . [*Reading*] It was in his father's brow. A measured crease that was always present, but deepened, not with concern as one would expect, but whenever the conversation shifted from him. Michael saw the shadow in that furrow grow darker, and he knew that soon his opening would have passed . . . It was not possible to express displeasure, even uncertainty in his father's presence, but a certain amount of honesty was required . . . a certain kind of communication, a language that played out in anecdotes and connotations, might . . .

TAYLOR: That's beautiful.

[*Lights fade as* KENT *continues reading.*]

# SCENE 4

[*The following morning. Morning lights filter in through windows. In the living room,* CHERYL *cleans up the mess from the night before, putting away the Trivial Pursuit board, placing glasses on a tray, etc.* TAYLOR, *wearing cutoffs, no bra, a faded tank top, and a bandanna, enters the kitchen from outside with a net and a jar, over which is a piece of paper. Setting the jar on the kitchen island, paper side down, she finds honey in the cabinet. She carefully spoons a teaspoonful onto the counter next to the jar, slides the paper out from beneath, and slides the jar on top of the honey. She looks for a long time and then very slowly removes the jar. A fly remains on the counter.* TAYLOR *slowly kneels, so that her head is level with the counter and observes the fly on the honey.* CHERYL *enters, unobserved, with a stack of dishes, places them on the counter, grabs a flyswatter from a hook in the pantry, returns, and unceremoniously swats* TAYLOR's *fly.*]

TAYLOR: What'd you do that for?

CHERYL: What? [*Noticing the sticky mess*] What the hell? . . .

TAYLOR: Didn't you see that I was . . . ?

CHERYL: You were? . . . Is this honey?

TAYLOR: Observing. The fly.

CHERYL: The fly? You put honey on the table?

[*Beat.*]

> To observe the . . . OK, OK. I, I didn't know. I'm sorry.

[*Beat.*]

> Why?

TAYLOR: It's what I do. Your specimens up here are a little different than the ones I see every day.

CHERYL: Specimens?

TAYLOR: Insects. I study them. The household fly mostly, but I collect, whatever, you know.

CHERYL: Sure.

[*Pause.*]

You always get up this early?

TAYLOR: The earlier the better.

CHERYL: I read your dad's book last night.

TAYLOR: Really? The whole thing?

CHERYL: What? You're surprised?

TAYLOR: No. It's just so long.

[*Beat.*]

And dense.

CHERYL: I thought it was good. He was pretty radical, huh?

TAYLOR: I guess. In his way.

CHERYL: I liked what he was saying about the economic ramifications of the slave trade . . .

[*Beat.*]

And how he makes it so specific . . .

[*Beat.*]

And traces the debt from shippers to traders to banks . . .

[*Pause.*]

You read it, right?

TAYLOR: Of course.

[*Four beats.*]

CHERYL: Well, what's your favorite part?

TAYLOR: Let me help you clean up this mess.

CHERYL: It's fine.

TAYLOR: I could start in on the dishes then, or . . .

CHERYL: No, thank you.

TAYLOR: I don't mind, really.

CHERYL: I said no thanks.

TAYLOR: Sorry.

[*Beat.*]

Do you get the paper here?

CHERYL: Yeah.

TAYLOR: Where?

CHERYL: What?

TAYLOR: The paper. Where do I get it?

CHERYL: It's on the porch if it came yet. Do you want me to . . . ?

TAYLOR: No, thanks. Thanks.

CHERYL: Sure.

[TAYLOR *exits to the porch.* CHERYL *loads the dishwasher.* TAYLOR *re-enters the kitchen loaded down with a huge stack of papers.*]

TAYLOR: Wow. Dr. LeVay gets everything.

CHERYL: Yeah, we call and have them start up a couple of weeks before they get here. He gets nervous if they're not waiting for him.

TAYLOR: Do you think he'd mind if I started in on them?

CHERYL: No.

TAYLOR: OK then. If I can't help clean up this mess . . .

[*Silence.*]

I'll just . . . OK.

[TAYLOR *fans papers out on the island.*]

Do you mind if I put on a pot of coffee?

CHERYL: I'll do it. I usually wait until the first person gets up.

TAYLOR: I can do it.

CHERYL: That's OK.

TAYLOR: I don't mind.

CHERYL: Decaf or regular?

TAYLOR: Whatever's easiest.

CHERYL: You've made coffee before, right?

TAYLOR: Sure.

CHERYL: So you know one is the same as the other, right?

TAYLOR: I'm sorry. Regular. I'll just take the papers, I'll just . . . OK then . . . yeah . . . OK.

[TAYLOR *backs out of the kitchen and exits to the living room with her papers.* CHERYL *puts the coffee on and begins making breakfast.* TAYLOR *settles on the couch in the living room and sorts papers, removing coverings, placing them in order in individual piles. This goes on for some time. All is quiet. Just when the lack of action is unnerving, the audience is startled by a loud knock on the door.* CHERYL *starts for it, but before she enters the living room* TAYLOR *speaks.*]

I've got it.

[TAYLOR *opens the door.* KIMBER *stands on the other side looking appropriately casual but notably put together, in stark contrast to* TAYLOR'*s cutoffs, braless faded tank top, and bandanna.*]

Oh, hello.

KIMBER: Hi. This is twenty-twenty Brayburry, isn't it?

TAYLOR: I don't know. There's no sign?

[TAYLOR *pokes her head out of the door.*]

KIMBER: Couldn't find it, no.

TAYLOR: This is the LeVay residence.

KIMBER: Good, good. I'm in the right place. Hi, I'm Kimber Davies. Flip's friend.

TAYLOR: Of course. He told us about you. That you were coming. Come in. Here, let me help with your—

KIMBER: You must be Cheryl. Flip's told me about you. Congratulations, about graduating . . .

TAYLOR: No. Taylor. Spoon, Kent. Harold, Flip's brother's fiancée.

KIMBER: I'm sorry. So nice to meet you.

TAYLOR: I thought you'd have an accent.

KIMBER: What?

TAYLOR: Oh. Anyway, I'm up before everyone and I was feeling a little . . . you know, like the new girl. I usually clean when I want to fit in, but that's Cheryl's job, so, I'm, I'm a little lost.

KIMBER: OK.

[*Pause.*]

So, uh . . . Is Flip here?

TAYLOR: I think they're all still asleep. We could wake them up, or . . .

[KIMBER *puts her suitcase by the stairs.*]

KIMBER: I can wait it out. Is there coffee?

TAYLOR [*crossing toward the kitchen with* KIMBER]: Yes . . . you can have regular or decaf as both are very easy to make . . .

[*As they enter the kitchen,* KENT *and* FLIP *bound down the stairs, both in boxers and T-shirts.*]

KENT: What's the hurry, man?

FLIP: I thought I heard the door.

KENT: So?

FLIP: Can't run interference from the bedroom.

[KENT *and* FLIP *remain in living room as the scene switches to the kitchen.*]

TAYLOR: Cheryl, this is Kimber.

KIMBER: Hi Cheryl, Flip's told me so much about—

CHERYL: Coffee's ready.

KIMBER: Congratulations on your—

CHERYL: Grapefruit's in the fridge. Thought I'd wait till they were up to put on the eggs. I better go get the . . .

[CHERYL *exits toward her bedroom while* TAYLOR *pulls mugs out of the cabinet and pours coffee.* KIMBER *looks in the fridge for cream.* KENT *and* FLIP *enter.*]

FLIP: You made it.

[FLIP *and* KIMBER *hug.*]

Were the directions OK, baby?

KIMBER: Oh fine. It was a long flight, bad air, you know, over the mountains.

FLIP: Poor baby.

KIMBER: Hey . . . nice shirt.

FLIP: This girl I know got it for me.

KIMBER: She has good taste.

FLIP: Yes, you do.

KENT: *Buongiorno, bella!*

KIMBER: Oh, OK then. *Buongiorno.*

FLIP: I'm sorry I haven't made introductions. Kimber this is . . .

KIMBER: You're Kent. Of course. Nice to meet you. I enjoyed your book.

KENT: You let her read it without asking . . .

FLIP: You've met Taylor then . . .

TAYLOR: Yeah. Yeah. We go way back. Coffee?

[DAD *enters the kitchen.*]

DAD: . . . Cheryl, you know who messed with my papers?

FLIP: Dad.

DAD [*seeing* KIMBER]: Oh, Buon giorno, Bella Signorina. Benvenuta a casa nostra. Lei e' piu', bella di tutti i fiori del mondo . . .*

[*Lights fade.*]


# SCENE 5

[*Later that evening.* TAYLOR, KENT, FLIP, KIMBER, *and* DAD *lounge in the living room. Lobster carcasses litter the coffee table. Drunken laughter fills the room.*]

KIMBER: Oh my God . . . Stop . . . Stop—

TAYLOR: I could eat lobster everyday.

KENT: You can.

TAYLOR: It's so good.

FLIP: Anything's good when you dip it in melted butter . . .

DAD: Taylor, you were telling us about . . .

FLIP: Yes . . . Taylor, please regale us with more amusing anecdotes.

TAYLOR: Have I been talking too much . . . It doesn't matter, I—

DAD: Your junior year . . .

---

*Oh, good day, beautiful girl. Welcome to our home. You are more beautiful than all the flowers in the world.

[TAYLOR *looks at* KENT.]

KENT: You don't have to—

TAYLOR: My junior year, college—

KIMBER: I'm sorry to interrupt. He really told you guys that I'm Italian?

TAYLOR: Yeah. But you are, right?

KIMBER: No. Straight-up WASPs.

FLIP: Your aunt has a pasta maker . . .

KENT: Let it go, man, you're busted.

FLIP: Mom would kick our asses if she saw us.

KENT: We eat at the dining room table.

FLIP: She flips out if you eat so much as a bologna sandwich on the couch.

DAD: And watch yourself, it'll be my ass if you leave crumbs.

KIMBER: Kent, I've been wanting to tell you how much I really enjoyed your novel.

TAYLOR: That's right, you read it.

[CHERYL *enters, clearing the table as conversation continues.*]

KIMBER: Yeah, it was really good.

[CHERYL *removes* KENT's *plate.*]

KENT [*to* KIMBER]: Thank you.

KIMBER AND CHERYL: You're welcome.

CHERYL: Oh.

KIMBER: It reminded me of some of my own family dynamics.

TAYLOR: Really?

CHERYL: There's a banana pudding if anyone's interested?

DAD: Oh, God bless you, Cheryl.

KIMBER: A good writer communicates across worlds by effectively communicating the specificity of his own world.

TAYLOR: I think the strength is in how universal the story is . . .

KENT: No, Taylor, I think she's right. It's only universal because I'm specific about the characters, the relationships . . .

TAYLOR [*to* KIMBER]: You were a lit major?

CHERYL: So, you all want dessert?

FLIP: Yes, thanks, Cheryl.

[CHERYL *exits.*]

KIMBER: Political science with a focus on African American studies undergrad . . . My dissertation was on achievement gap issues . . . I'm just saying, I was moved. I'm the youngest too . . .

DAD: So, we're talking about Kent's book? I thought Taylor was saying something about . . .

KENT: That youngest child thing is a trip, isn't it!?

KIMBER: Oh God, yes. But also your imagery is amazing, really out of this world, and the ease with which you segue from one setting to the next. And the landscape, like a metaphor for the fragile state of Michael's psyche.

DAD: Well, since we haven't all read it, perhaps we can talk about something—

KENT: I don't know if I'd call it "fragile." I think he's stronger than you might—

KIMBER: Absolutely, I misspoke. He's terribly strong. But there's a vulnerability that's so attractive—

TAYLOR: Attractive?

KIMBER: Appealing.

TAYLOR: Appealing.

KIMBER: Is there a lot of you in Michael?

KENT: Well, certainly the *appealing* parts.

[KENT *and* KIMBER *share a laugh.*]

FLIP: Yeah . . . so, this is nice. Dad, where the hell is Mom? This is crazy . . .

KENT: Wasn't she coming this morning?

FLIP: I'm calling, where's my phone? . . .

[FLIP *looks for his cell phone.*]

It's upstairs. Kimber, could you run up and . . .

DAD [*to* KIMBER]: Sit. [*To* FLIP *and* KENT] Don't disturb your mother . . . For years you guys get here whenever the hell it works with your schedule . . . You can't afford her that much latitude? [*To* TAYLOR] Taylor, you started a story that we so rudely interrupted . . .

TAYLOR: What?

DAD: Your junior year . . .

[CHERYL *returns with a tray of dessert dishes. She dishes out the pudding and serves it as the conversation continues.*]

TAYLOR: I don't know . . . It's not such a big deal. Well, I sat down to play a game of solitaire and I didn't stop for the rest of the semester.

KIMBER: Cards?

TAYLOR: No.

KENT: Computer. It was the first semester of her junior year and . . .

TAYLOR: And I used my work-study money to get this cute little laptop and it came with solitaire.

KIMBER: But you graduated early, right?

KENT: She did, and with honors. You don't have to go into this honey.

KIMBER: Then I don't get it. What was the problem?

TAYLOR: It's not a problem, really. I'm not ashamed. I had a women's studies class that morning. One of these really intimate, little, what do they call them, a little honors seminar. We were so liberal and smart. It was like eight white girls named Becky . . . [*To* KIMBER] No offense. I'm sure they had different names.

KIMBER: None taken.

TAYLOR: . . . And a gay white guy and this quiet little Asian girl and me. And they're talking about Weber's theories on social dominance and they've built this hypothetical utopian society—

FLIP: Oh yeah, economy and society . . .

TAYLOR: Wow, OK. So, [*to* FLIP] unlike anything Weber could have conceived of, this society would have no men, and so would be perfect. I look over at Tofer . . .

KIMBER: Tofer?

TAYLOR: The gay white guy. And I'm waiting for him to say something . . . But we've all had enough psych to know what happens to the power dynamics when you're the only one.

KIMBER: Yeah.

[CHERYL *hands* TAYLOR *her bowl.* TAYLOR *overthanks her. Throughout the following,* CHERYL *half cleans, moving from kitchen to living room, sometimes pausing, absorbed in the conversation.*]

TAYLOR: Thank you, Cheryl. So, Tofer's quiet. And I say, "Is your utopia free of color distinctions?" And I'm careful not to look at the Asian girl.

DAD: Fucked 'em up, hey?

KENT: Dad.

DAD: What? She fucked 'em up.

KIMBER: Woman.

TAYLOR: What?

KIMBER: The Asian *woman.*

TAYLOR: Fine, I'm careful not to look at the Asian *woman,* because, I don't know, I don't want to assume that she's got a similar worldview.

FLIP: I've dated Asian girls. They're down.

KIMBER: Women.

TAYLOR: It's all relative. From where I sit the bulk of the racial stuff they get is that people assume they're smart, guys want to date them, and they fit all of the shoes on the sales rack.

KIMBER: Well, as long as there's no hypocrisy in your lamentations.

FLIP: No, no, baby, that's not hypocrisy; that's straight-up racism.

TAYLOR: And one of the Beckys says, "Like, what do you mean, color distinctions?" And I look at the professor, with her pageboy-Birkenstock-unshaved ass and she's not giving it up. So I'm on. And I explain that not only is it problematic that we haven't stopped to consider racial tensions in our now female-dominated society, but we haven't even begun to consider class.

FLIP: I'm not sure that class matters.

DAD: Son, I raised you better than that. This house has been full of octoroons and quadroons for three generations and you think our loving white neighbors wouldn't rather we move over to the bluffs with the other Negros? Cheryl, could you top me off please, dear?

[CHERYL *pours him more wine.*]

You can just leave the bottle . . . thanks.

FLIP: Well I haven't noticed it matters so much how much money you have. If you're a nigger folks gonna see a nigger. Don't you think, Cheryl?

[CHERYL *is about to answer when* KIMBER *cuts her off.*]

KIMBER: But surely money creates a social buffer?

DAD: Taylor was talking.

FLIP: Taylor is always talking.

DAD: I want to know. What happened?

TAYLOR: Really, it's hard to remember, it's all sort of blurred together.

FLIP: Like she hasn't told this a million times . . .

TAYLOR: Fine. So one of the Beckys gets quite hostile, and then just downright ignorant, and eventually she was saying that if it was a utopian society, there would be only one dominant race, and the teacher is agreeing, and I'm trying to show them that this would not be a utopian society, that this would be the Third Reich . . . and the Asian girl is saying it's just for purposes of discussion, but she's clearly very upset. But this is the kicker: I get a call from the professor the next day. She'd like to apologize for letting things get out of control. She's pretty sure that at some point things may have become racist, and I say, "I think it started when you decided to teach a class called Feminist Voices of the Twentieth Century and include no women of color."

KIMBER: That's awful.

TAYLOR: Well, she explains there really aren't women of color accepted in the canon of hard feminist discourse.

KIMBER: What about bell hooks?

TAYLOR: That's what I said!

[KIMBER *goes for a high five, but* TAYLOR *leaves her hanging.*]

And then she misquotes my dad back to me as if he would support such nonsense. He would, but still, she doesn't know that.

[*The telephone rings.* CHERYL *exits to kitchen to get it.*]

I can wait, if you need to . . .

DAD: Cheryl'll get it.

[CHERYL *answers the phone in the kitchen.*]

CHERYL: Hello . . . Oh . . . sure, one second . . .

[*The conversation continues in the living room.*]

DAD: Go on.

TAYLOR: I guess it was the last straw or something. That was it. I'd been fighting pretty much the same battle since high school.

KIMBER: Seems you would have learned to put it in perspective.

TAYLOR: Perspective? I was tired. I was supposed to be getting an education, but instead, I'm teaching Cultural Sensitivity 101 every time I turn around, and have been since like, third grade. So I go home and take a shower and turn on my little laptop, and it's so pretty and I select Vegas style . . . and I play and sleep and occasionally eat and I don't stop playing.

[CHERYL *pokes her head out of the kitchen.*]

CHERYL: Dr. LeVay, it's Mrs. LeVay . . .

DAD: Tell her I'll call her back.

CHERYL: She says it's . . .

DAD: What did I say, Cheryl?

CHERYL: Yes, sir.

[CHERYL *exits.*]

KENT: Dad!

DAD: What?

[FLIP *and* KENT *exchange a look: this is strange behavior from* DAD.]

FLIP: So you're saying white feminist discourse precipitated a nervous breakdown?

KIMBER: Flip.

KENT: She's just telling you what happened to—

DAD: I think she's saying the white people drove her out of her ravin'-ass mind.

[CHERYL *enters again, continues clearing off table, pouring coffee or some such.*]

TAYLOR: Yes, Dr. LeVay, the white people finally drove me crazy. But I didn't know I was crazy. I thought I was just really liking solitaire. Didn't matter I was a straight A student. No one missed me, the only raisin in the oatmeal, the only speck of nutmeg on the eggnog.

KIMBER: Maybe they were grateful for your absence.

[*Beat.*]

I don't mean that badly.

TAYLOR: Sure you do.

KIMBER: No, no, all I'm saying, really, is that it's hard to have someone rubbing your nose in your own bullshit all the time. It sounds like you can be relentless.

TAYLOR: I don't know. I think you can be relentless and keep chipping away at the bullshit, or you can be passive and confused and lose your mind.

FLIP: You lost it anyway.

KIMBER: Flip.

FLIP: Stop Flipping me. This is ridiculous, and we're indulging her. Come on, we all went to good schools.

TAYLOR: By "good" you mean white?

FLIP: There were black folks like me at Exeter and Harvard.

TAYLOR: That was my problem. The black folks at Harvard were like you.

FLIP: What?

TAYLOR: Come on. I couldn't have hung out with your crowd. You were flying to Aspen for the weekend and driving around in SUVs and shit.

FLIP: I had Dad's old Saab.

TAYLOR: Oh, well then.

KENT: Cheryl.

[CHERYL *is caught off guard.*]

CHERYL: Oh . . . Coffee?

[CHERYL *collects wine glasses.*]

KENT: No, thank you. But Cheryl, you went to a nice school.

DAD: Cheryl had a scholarship at the best high school in Manhattan.

TAYLOR: That must have been a trip.

CHERYL: It was alright. The classes were amazing.

TAYLOR: Didn't you feel . . . out of place?

CHERYL: Why?

TAYLOR: It just seems like it would be a difficult transition.

CHERYL: From what? I went to grade school. School is school.

KIMBER: Did you have friends?

CHERYL: I wasn't trying to have friends. I didn't want to be friends with them people. I just wanted to get good grades so I could get a scholarship to college.

DAD: A black girl with a diploma from that school can go anywhere.

KIMBER: Here's what I don't get, Taylor . . . I mean, I work with black and Latino kids in the inner city . . .

TAYLOR: I know you didn't just . . .

KENT: Honey . . . Come on . . .

KIMBER: That was my dissertation, around inequalities in education. Anyway, I have a hard time feeling sorry for you, daughter of a famous intellectual.

TAYLOR: Just by birth. He got a new family.

KIMBER: Anyway, I swear, some of the places these kids live, it's like a third-world country.

TAYLOR: And I guess you saw plenty of those in the Peace Corps after you bummed around Europe.

KENT: Taylor!

TAYLOR [to KENT]: What?! She doesn't know me . . . [To KIMBER] You don't know me . . .

FLIP [to KENT]: Can you shut her up?

KIMBER [to FLIP]: That's OK, honey. I'm OK. [To TAYLOR] Yes, so you know me well. Yes, Europe—Peace Corps. And so help me here, there you were, at this privileged institution, with your famous dad and your new laptop to soothe yourself, and you're upset because some stupid sorority chicks are mean to you?

KENT [under his breath]: Oh God.

CHERYL: Seems like a fair question.

[Long pause.]

So, I'm gonna . . . OK . . . there's coffee, decaf and regular, in the kitchen.

[CHERYL *stops before getting to the kitchen, now interested in* TAYLOR's *tirade.*]

TAYLOR: No, Kimber. I was upset because people like you can't see it. Your inner-city kids aren't supposed to succeed . . . As long as they can stay ignorant and dependent on you, they won't have to mess up the white spaces. They let one or two of us in who've had enough privilege to almost play the game. Just enough to make us think we're special. It's a grand mindfuck. Then Kimmy here goes slummin' for five minutes and knows all about it.

[*To* KIMBER] You can kiss my black ass is what you can do with your I'm-such-a-Goddamn-saint-inner-fuckin'-sanctum-of-rebellious-white-liberal bullshit. Don't you ever come to me like that. You need to get your white ass out of my world, or keep your hippie drivel to your own damn self . . . [*Mumbling to herself*] Fuckin' I'll show Dad what happens if he won't notice me . . . I'm too deep for cotillions, I'll fuck black and show them all, bitch.

[*Long, long, long pause.* TAYLOR *has risen and stands facing a room of shocked faces. Her bravado melts into shame. She sits.*]

OK. Did I say that out loud?

[*Long pause.*]

[*To* KIMBER] So. So grateful to you, though, for fighting the good fight. On behalf of my downtrodden brothas and sistahs, I thank you.

[TAYLOR *rises.*]

Dr. LeVay . . .

DAD: Joseph.

TAYLOR: Joseph, Flip, Kim-*berly*, it's been a wonderful evening. Thank you. Cheryl, it was delicious, thank you. If you don't mind Spoon, I'd like to get some fresh air.

KENT: I don't mind.

[KENT *doesn't budge.*]

TAYLOR: I thought you'd join me.

[KENT *is frozen, completely unsure of what to do.*]

DAD: Go on, son.

[KENT *and* TAYLOR *exit to the kitchen. There is a long moment of silence.*]

CHERYL: Should I get Mrs. LeVay on the phone for you now?

DAD: No. Thank you, Cheryl. No, and don't ask again. Understood?

[CHERYL *begins exiting toward the kitchen, clearing things as she goes.*]

Parcheesi?

FLIP: I'll get the board.

KIMBER: I'm turning in . . . Goodnight, Dr. LeVay.

[KIMBER *kisses* FLIP *and starts to make her way upstairs as the scene switches to the kitchen.*]

TAYLOR: Goddamnit. That's not what I'm saying, and you know it.

*[Scene switches to the living room.]*

FLIP: You want me to come up with you?

KIMBER: No . . . I'm OK. Really . . .

*[She exits up stairs.* KENT *sets up the Parcheesi board near* DAD's *chair. Scene switches to the kitchen. Awkward silence as* CHERYL *enters the kitchen.]*

KENT: Could you excuse us, Cheryl?

TAYLOR: Don't talk to her like that.

CHERYL: No, no. That's cool. I'm cool.

*[*CHERYL *exits into her bedroom.]*

TAYLOR: All that I ask is that you have my back.

KENT: This is my family, Taylor.

TAYLOR: I'm your family.

KENT: Not yet.

TAYLOR: So this is some sort of test? Can the low-class girl hang in the big leagues . . . ?

KENT: That's ridiculous.

TAYLOR: Is it?

KENT: Is that what this is about? Have you lost your mind? You grew up solidly upper middle class—

TAYLOR: Lower middle class . . . and nothing was solid.

KENT: You had entrée.

TAYLOR: Entrée to what? Places I couldn't afford to go? Forget it. Why didn't you help me out? You heard her. I thought we were on the same side?

KENT: I didn't say I disagree with you.

TAYLOR: You didn't *say* anything.

KENT: There was nothing to say. I didn't know you were going to curse the girl out.

TAYLOR: That's ridiculous. It was a heated discussion. I just said what was on my mind. She's way out of line with that "I worked in the inner-city" bullshit.

KENT: But you're not from the inner city.

TAYLOR: I'd might as well be.

KENT: What?

TAYLOR: It was just me and my mom and an apartment full of books. Books, and opportunity . . . never enough money. And my dad wasn't giving it up . . . His family had a driver, a Porsche, an SUV . . . and we're trying to get the Neon out of repo . . .

KENT: What does this have to do with her?

TAYLOR: Who?

KENT: Kimber.

TAYLOR: . . . Like she knows what it feels like to be me . . .

KENT: I don't know what it feels like to be you!

[*Pause. Phone rings.* KENT *gets it.*]

Ma? . . . Oh, Ms. Ellie. It's Spoon, Kent. Yeah. I can get her. [*Walking toward* CHERYL*'s room*] Cheryl! [*To Ms. Ellie*] I'm sorry to hear you're under the weather.

[*Beat.*]

I don't know where she is. Hold on. Sure. [*Poking his head out of the kitchen*] Cheryl!

[CHERYL *enters from the bedroom, grabs the phone from* KENT, *and returns to her bedroom.*]

[*To* TAYLOR] Look. You're upset. I don't know what I am. Can we just walk into town and get a drink or something? Please?

TAYLOR: No. I just don't understand why you're acting like this!

KENT: Lower your voice.

[KENT *drags* TAYLOR *out to the porch.*]

Like what?

[*Beat.*]

Can't we just get away from the house and talk for a minute?

TAYLOR: What do you have to say that you can't say here?

KENT: You acted all worried about "Will my mother like you?" and shit . . . You keep it up, I don't know if I still like you. Damn. What's gotten into you?

TAYLOR: I don't know. Really. I don't. You know my dad got a place over in Oak Bluffs? I'm sure they still come. That's why I don't want to go out. I'm scared to death of running into his family. It's crazy, I know. But, I think this was a bad idea. It's too close, and it brings up all this stuff. One summer my mom gets this fellowship to teach in Japan, just for a month, and she asks my dad if I can spend part of the summer with him. You know what he said? "It would be too complicated. We're going to the Vineyard." Just like that, the Vineyard.

KENT: Sssshhhh.

[KENT *pulls* TAYLOR *into an embrace.*]

TAYLOR: You just need me to hold it together, huh?

KENT: Sweetheart, I'm just working to hold it together myself.

TAYLOR: You wanna come to bed . . .

KENT: Naw . . . I need a little time. I'll catch you later.

TAYLOR: You're mad?

KENT: I'm . . . needing a little time . . .

[KENT *disengages from the hug and exits around the porch and into the dark. Scene switches to the kitchen, where* FLIP *meanwhile has deserted* DAD, *who has fallen asleep in the chair, and has entered the kitchen and is eating a large piece of chocolate cake with gusto. He has not turned on the light and eats only by the light of the open refrigerator.* TAYLOR *enters the kitchen.*]

TAYLOR: Oh my God. You scared the crap out of me.

FLIP: God's so formal. Call me Flip. Cake?

[TAYLOR *takes a plate from the cupboard, helping herself to a piece of cake.*]

TAYLOR: It's late. Shouldn't you be in bed with Ember?

FLIP: Kimber.

TAYLOR: Whatever.

FLIP: No, she's probably taking a bubble bath, preparing for my arrival.

TAYLOR: You're gross . . .

FLIP: Why are you being such a bitch?

TAYLOR: I'm being very nice.

FLIP: I'm being frank.

TAYLOR: Well, God, I thought you said to call you Flip.

FLIP: Why you so hard on my girl? What gives?

TAYLOR: It's late for confrontation. And you know what gives.

FLIP: I understand that we're all supposed to be adults. And you seem to have no social restraint, which concerns me, since you're going to be my little brother's wife.

TAYLOR: Hey, be nice. I'm almost your sister.

FLIP: No such thing. Right now you're just the gold digger engaged to my brother.

TAYLOR [truly taken aback]: I'm sorry, I thought we were just sparring, and this just turned into something so, ugly, and I don't know how to . . . I didn't expect . . . Excuse me . . .

[TAYLOR begins to exit.]

FLIP: It's a nice evening. Shouldn't you be upstairs with your man?

TAYLOR: I'm sorry?

FLIP: Vacation, alcove room, warm fresh air, white linen curtains billowing . . . you know. What are you doing down here?

TAYLOR: I'm still up. Besides, we're in separate rooms. Aren't you and Kimber?

FLIP: I'm thirty-seven. I get to sleep with whomever I please.

[*Beat.*]

I wouldn't take it personally. Kent's the baby. They're protective.

TAYLOR: With me he's no baby.

FLIP: Um . . .

TAYLOR: I love Spoon.

FLIP: Trying to convince someone?

[FLIP *gets up from the table and walks toward door to living room.*]

TAYLOR: You're just gonna leave that? Your plate. On the counter?

FLIP: Cheryl'll get it.

TAYLOR: I got it.

[TAYLOR *clears the table and rinses the plates. Pause.*]

Why didn't you ever call me?

FLIP: I'm sorry?

TAYLOR: You never called.

FLIP: No. That was six years ago . . . Let it go. Damn. 'Sides, you're supposed to be in love with my brother.

TAYLOR: I just thought you would say something.

FLIP: So, you wanted me, say, at dinner, over the mashed potatoes, to
say, What do you call him? . . . Oh yeah, Spoon. "Spoon . . . I
fucked the brains out of our girl here in Atlanta six years ago."

TAYLOR: I didn't know you fucked my brains out. I thought it meant something. Right after the solitaire episode, I rented this beater and drove to the art fair in Atlanta and I met you.

And you were nice to me. Really nice. And you bought me dinner, and we talked and laughed, for hours. And you made me feel so comfortable. Like I had never felt comfortable with anyone before. Except for when I met Spoon. You made me feel . . . wanted. You did things that no one had ever done, to me. Like you wanted to . . .

FLIP: Don't embarrass yourself.

TAYLOR: The truth embarrasses you?

FLIP: Why do you women do that? Like some damn *The Way We Were* Sunday flick fantasy. You, you're a beautiful, smart woman, and you'll lay down with just anyone who's a little bit nice to you for gumbo and a cheap glass of wine?

TAYLOR: You misunderstand.

FLIP: Oh, I think I understand perfectly. On this day, this beautiful day, I see this woman who is so young and firm and beautiful, and not in need of alteration. And she doesn't know that I'm a plastic surgeon. And, after talking to her for a few minutes, I see that she wouldn't care anyway. This girl likes to play with bugs. And that's amusing to me. And she's witty and charming and hasn't even asked me what I do. So, I ask her out. And I take her to a dive, good food, but a dive. And she's so happy just to be there with me. And I ask her back to my place, really just to talk. 'Cause I'm thinkin' she's . . . special. But I find that she's no different. Just so willing to lay down and give herself over, to someone as undeserving as I. I didn't have to work for it. So yes, I fuck her brains out . . . and forget all about her. Until this bitter, bitter girl comes home with my brother.

TAYLOR: You'll never be happy.

FLIP: Are you? Now?

TAYLOR: Yes.

[FLIP *pulls* TAYLOR *toward him.*]

FLIP: Does he look into your eyes? Does he know where, how, to touch your soul? Can he make you want things? Unspeakable things . . .

TAYLOR: He touches my heart.

FLIP: Can he make you beg . . . ? Will you touch yourself for him . . . ? Will you . . . ?

TAYLOR: He makes me safe.

FLIP: Keep saying that to yourself.

[DAD *enters from the living room, surveys the scene, and says nothing.* TAYLOR *moves casually away from* FLIP, *turning her back to both, searching through cabinets for nothing.* DAD *pours himself a cup of coffee and exits. A short pause.* DAD *enters again.*]

DAD: I expect one of you will be joining me shortly in the living room for a game of backgammon.

[DAD *exits.*]

TAYLOR: I don't know what you think that was, but I'm just fine.

FLIP: Tonight, I expect you'll be making your way across the hall to the alcove room. When he touches you, you think of me. I promise you the most intense orgasm of your life.

TAYLOR: And when I do have that orgasm, it'll be his name on my lips, but, and this is the part you don't get . . . It'll be mine on his. Because he knows me. Better than I know myself. Maybe if you weren't so afraid you'd find that kind of love one day. Guess you owe your dad a game of backgammon. I'm going to bed.

[TAYLOR *exits.*]

# ACT 2

## SCENE 1

[*Early the next morning.* DAD *sits on the porch with a pipe, reading a book.* CHERYL *enters the kitchen from her room, on a cell phone. She's been crying. She makes coffee.*]

CHERYL: . . . Ma, I don't see there's anything else to talk about . . . No. No! I'm not being disrespectful. I just can't believe you sent me here and you knew you was gone tell me the truth. Now? That's not right. All you had to do was say that you're not coming. Why you have to drag my ass into this? No. I'm sorry. No, *ma'am.* My *butt.* Wait a minute, I lost count.

[*She pours the coffee she's spooned into the filter back into the coffee can and starts again.*]

Three, four, five, six.

[*Pause.*]

74

I'm sorry you're sick . . . but they could of called dial-a-frickin'-maid.

[*Beat.*]

It's not a swear word.

[*Beat.*]

Are you serious?

[*Beat.*]

Fine. Melon, prosciutto, deviled eggs, berries, cereal, and yogurt.

[*Pause.* CHERYL *breaks down.* KIMBER *has entered, unseen. She stands just in the doorway.*]

Eighteen years, Ma. That's a really long time to just now say your daddy didn't die in Desert Storm. I'm all by myself cleanin' up after the man, an' you choose now to say, "Guess who your daddy is?" That's crazy. Does he know?

[*Beat.*]

I don't even know what to . . . [*Seeing* KIMBER *in doorway*] Oh my God. Oh shit . . . I gotta go.

[KIMBER *enters in T-shirt and pajama bottoms. She finds a napkin and hands it to* CHERYL. CHERYL *blows her nose. Long silence.*]

I'm gonna hear about that. That I said "shit."

KIMBER: "Shit" seems appropriate somehow.

CHERYL: So you heard.

KIMBER: I think so.

CHERYL: Please don't say nothin' to nobody . . .

KIMBER: I wouldn't.

[CHERYL *pours herself coffee.*]

CHERYL: Wakes me up, says, "Guess who yo' daddy is," and asks what I'm serving for breakfast. You know, all these years, my whole life, I been saying goodnight to a picture of a man in a uniform who's s'posed to be my daddy. But no . . . uh-uh, and wait, wait, wait, then she tells me where the eggcups are. Who the fuck uses eggcups? They all crazy. I don't know what to do.

KIMBER: Are you asking me?

CHERYL: I don't see no one else's bony white ass up in here.

KIMBER [*looking at her butt*]: Thank you. Pilates.

CHERYL: You look like a princess, but you're pretty tough, aren't you?

KIMBER: Yeah.

CHERYL: No. I don't want advice. I gotta sit with it for a little while.

[*Pause.*]

I guess you can say something, about something. Since you're here.

KIMBER: I guess I could tell you my daddy shit . . . but it's complicated and I don't want to. Let's see. What we don't talk about in my family. My grandmother's brother married an Irish immigrant. In my world that's beyond unacceptable.

CHERYL: Sort of puts the whole Flip thing in perspective, don't it?

KIMBER: . . . Someone fell in love with someone they weren't supposed to . . . a whole branch of the family we don't acknowledge. I watched Grandma, loving, sweet, philanthropic, Chanel-and-pearl-wearing old lady, walk past nieces and nephews on the street without a word. Just cut 'em out. No one questioned it. I didn't even. And these are people who vote family values. Why am I telling you this?

CHERYL: I sure don't know, 'cause it doesn't hold a candle.

KIMBER: No, it doesn't. It's just that I loved my grandmother. And even when I thought she was the meanest piece of work in Ferragamo, she was still the only one who saw me.

[*Pause.*]

Mostly, I didn't know what else to say. To you. I should maybe have just said I'm sorry.

CHERYL: Yeah. You should have.

[FLIP *enters.*]

FLIP: Morning.

[*He kisses* KIMBER *on the head and makes a beeline to the coffee.*]

KIMBER: Oh, hey, honey.

FLIP: Sleep well?

KIMBER: Like a log.

FLIP: I bet you did . . . [*Noticing* CHERYL] Hey, Cheryl. You OK?

[TAYLOR *enters with a small crate of glass jars.*]

CHERYL: Uh-huh . . .

[CHERYL *busies herself at the kitchen sink. Then she searches in the fridge for nothing.*]

TAYLOR: Morning.

KIMBER: Morning.

[TAYLOR *makes a beeline for the coffee. She bumps into* FLIP, *retreats, awkwardly circling around the room and reapproaching from another direction.* CHERYL *busies herself and then exits to her room.* KIMBER *watches all of the players.*]

FLIP [*to* KIMBER]: Hey baby, look what I got.

[*He holds up a green jar of Revlon Oil Sheen.*]

The dark-green kind. Found it in the medicine cabinet.

[*Beat.*]

Please?

[KIMBER *and* FLIP *exit to the living room.*]

I'll be right back baby . . . Forgot my coffee.

[TAYLOR *fixes her coffee and begins to struggle with juggling coffee and crate, about to exit to the back porch.* FLIP *reenters the kitchen.*]

[*To* TAYLOR] Yeah . . . uh, about last night . . . I don't know what that was . . .

TAYLOR: Is that an apology?

FLIP: Yeah.

TAYLOR: OK.

[TAYLOR *and* FLIP *exit the kitchen at the same time,* TAYLOR *to the porch and* FLIP *back to the living room.* TAYLOR *sees* DAD.]

Oh, good morning. Everyone's up so early.

[*Scene switches to the living room.*]

KIMBER: Where's your coffee?

FLIP: What?

KIMBER: You went to get . . .

FLIP: Right . . .

[FLIP *reenters the kitchen, retrieves his cup, and goes back to the living room. While* FLIP *gets coffee,* TAYLOR *and* DAD *talk on the porch.*]

TAYLOR: You look so peaceful [*starting to leave*], I don't want to . . .

DAD: Wait. Stay. It's a big porch.

TAYLOR: OK.

[*In the living room,* KIMBER *sits on the couch, with* FLIP *between her legs on the floor.*]

KIMBER: You have a comb?

FLIP: If you really loved me you'd use your fingers . . .

[*On the porch,* TAYLOR *is lining her jars up on the rail.*]

DAD: . . . I was just thumbing through another of your dad's . . . let's see . . . [*Turning the book over*] *A Legacy of Rage.*

TAYLOR: Um . . . You smoke?

DAD: Makes me look smart.

[*Beat.*]

Where's your Spoon?

TAYLOR: I don't know. Can't you get mouth cancer or something?

DAD: You'll get cancer a lot faster carrying around all that stuff you got going on in there. Also, no tobacco. I just pose with it. [*Gesturing to a row of jars on the porch rail*] What do you have there?

TAYLOR: I like to collect samples from places I've never been. Look at this. Isn't he beautiful . . . ?

DAD: Is that a dragonfly?

TAYLOR: A damselfly. Same family, but smaller. The air force has been studying these for years. They stop on a dime, change direction, go up, down . . . It's amazing. And you know they can reproduce in flight . . .

DAD [*laughing*]: . . . I tried that once . . .

TAYLOR: Dr. LeVay! Sometimes I think they know we're watching . . .

[*In the living room,* FLIP *grabs* KIMBER'S *leg.*]

FLIP: . . . Nice. I like your legs . . . nice, meaty . . . something you can bite into. This is a leg.

KIMBER: A nice helping of white meat . . .

FLIP: Honey, legs, that's dark meat. 'Sides, if it's nice and soft, and plump, something you can sink your teeth into, hue becomes arbitrary.

[*Pause.*]

DAD [*to* TAYLOR] AND FLIP [*to* KIMBER]: You enjoying yourself?

TAYLOR AND KIMBER: You're serious?

[*Scene switches to the porch.*]

TAYLOR: It's OK I guess.

DAD: You guess? I don't believe all that festering in there is about that nice girl we've got visiting us.

[*Scene switches to the living room.*]

FLIP: I mean surely you're not letting that girl ruin your stay. I don't bring just anyone up here.

KIMBER: I find that hard to believe.

FLIP: What, that you're not just anyone . . . ?

KIMBER: Please, this is all part of your mac-daddy package . . . the old pictures of you on the fridge, the cute little brother . . . a charming father . . . all part of a deeper kind of seduction.

FLIP: Yeah, maybe.

[*Scene switches to the porch.*]

DAD: So what's bothering you?

TAYLOR: It's not her . . .

DAD: It's not?

TAYLOR: I just find it exhausting never having a space that's all mine.

DAD: All yours?

TAYLOR: Well, I got here, and this incredible house, and all these beautiful black folks . . . I've never been on the inside of all of this, not like this. And it feels good . . . like, really good. Like right. But it's hard, it's scary, because, you know, I wanna make a good impression, and it's hard meeting the folks, the family. And then she walks in, like, like, no big deal.

DAD [*laughing*]: Seriously you think she's not sweatin'?

[*Scene switches to the living room.*]

KIMBER: I could care less if she likes me. Really . . . Just, tell me something.

FLIP: Yeah?

KIMBER: When did you and Taylor hit it?

FLIP: Hit it?

KIMBER: Flip . . . I can tell. I can feel it. And you don't think Spoon can?

FLIP: You're trippin'.

KIMBER: That's why she came all out-the-box on me . . .

FLIP: You've gotta stop talking like your kids.

KIMBER: You know what I'm saying . . . That wasn't about socioeconomics . . . That was about boys.

FLIP: What'd I tell you about that word? Can't be callin' a black man "boy."

KIMBER: Men. Look . . . we don't have the kind of thing that makes it OK for me to be jealous. So fine, I'm not jealous. But something's off and I think your brother deserves better.

[*Beat.*]

FLIP: Can you get my shoulders?

[KIMBER *starts massaging his shoulders. Scene switches to the porch.*]

DAD: She doesn't care.

TAYLOR: What?

DAD: You want to be liked. That's a hard road to go. Flip's girl doesn't care.

TAYLOR: She's never had to. The world stops for women like that.

FLIP [*in the living room, to* KIMBER] AND DAD [*on the porch, to* TAYLOR]: You're jealous . . .

TAYLOR [*on the porch*] AND KIMBER [*in the living room*]: I'm not jealous!

[*Scene switches to the living room.*]

KIMBER: I'm not . . .

FLIP: Ow!

[*Scene switches to the porch.*]

TAYLOR: You know how we look at flies? I mean, you know you can't just follow a fly around with a video cam, it's too fast. Film, even digital, can't pick up the nuances of a fly in motion. So, we glue a fly to a stick.

DAD: Really?

TAYLOR: Yeah. Pretty much a popsicle stick, with Krazy Glue. Plain ole Krazy Glue. And we hold the stick in front of a projection screen with three sides, like those Omnimax films, right? And we film his wing adjustments as we project objects coming at him. Isn't that crazy? Then we just throw it away and study the digital film images.

DAD: I think your biggest problem is you're freakishly smart and maybe a little weird. I could do a little operation and stop that brain of yours from spinning all the time.

TAYLOR: Is that what you think I need?

DAD: I don't know, I'm not a rocket scientist; I'm just a neurosurgeon.

[*They sit in silence for a moment. She goes back to examining her fly. Scene switches to the living room, where* CHERYL *enters.*]

CHERYL: Oh . . . Uhhhh . . . Have you seen Dr. LeVay?

FLIP: Isn't he on the porch? . . .

[CHERYL *stands awkwardly and starts to leave.*]

It's OK, Cheryl. We haven't had time to visit. Come, have a seat.

CHERYL: That's OK.

KIMBER: No, join us.

CHERYL: Uh . . . no . . . I still have to . . .

[CHERYL *exits into the kitchen.*]

KIMBER: She doesn't like me.

FLIP: No. She doesn't. Surely you're not jealous of jailbait?

KIMBER: She's got the biggest crush . . .

FLIP: Of course she does . . . Come here, bucket head.

KIMBER: Skillet head.

FLIP: Here, let me rub your feet.

KIMBER: Really?

FLIP: Yeah . . .

KIMBER: Oh, right there . . . To the left. Yeah.

[*A moment of silence while he rubs her feet.*]

FLIP: This is nice.

KIMBER: We should do more of this.

FLIP: This isn't what we do.

KIMBER: We fuck and pretend people don't hate us for it.

FLIP: We fuck and get off on that people hate us for it.

[KIMBER *removes herself.*]

KIMBER: You know Taylor's right. I was looking forward to taking you to the club and kissing you on the tennis court, and swimming in the pool—

FLIP: I'll play. No problem.

KIMBER: It's not fun anymore. Never was. It's really a lot like Taylor, just picking a fight because it's there.

FLIP: That's not what Taylor does.

KIMBER: See.

FLIP: I'm not defending her. I'm the last to defend her . . . but she usually has a point.

[*Beat.*]

KIMBER: Usually?

FLIP: She just needs to chill a little bit. Look . . . I'll be part of your whole revenge weekend thing with your family if you want.

KIMBER: But that's my point. I don't want that anymore.

FLIP: What the hell do you want?

KIMBER: The house, the family, you in this context, it got me.

FLIP: So what do you want?

KIMBER: Something normal. I want to go out to dinner, and not have sex after, and wake up on Sunday morning and put a baseball cap on and walk to Starbucks in our sweatpants and get the paper and come home and make love, and cram the book reviews because we have a dinner party that evening. I want to go to that party and pretend we read the books and talk about pretentious things and then laugh about the pretension on the ride home, and make love and set the alarm and go to work.

FLIP: I can't do that.

KIMBER: I know.

FLIP: But I told you, I don't do that.

KIMBER: I know.

FLIP: You said you didn't want that. I thought you were happy.

KIMBER: I was.

[KIMBER *rises and begins walking upstairs.*]

I am happy. I don't know.

[KIMBER *exits up the stairs, then comes back down and leans over the banister.*]

Tell you what I do know. Keep that bitch away from me or I'm gonna bust some moves, if you know what I mean.

FLIP: Awe sooky-sooky now . . . show me wha chu gone do?

[KIMBER *does a karate kick.* FLIP *goes toward the stairs, throws her over his shoulder, and carries her up the stairs. Scene switches to the porch, where* TAYLOR *and* DAD *are still talking.*]

TAYLOR: Does the idea of your family getting diluted piss you off, a little?

DAD [*amused*]: Diluted?

TAYLOR: Yeah.

DAD: Clearly there's a little cream in your coffee.

[*Beat.*]

Sweetie, if it wasn't for all that dilution, you think my wife's people would have this house? Don't you know most of the black folks got anything now, got it 'cause somewhere along the way somebody got raped in a kitchen. Don't look at me like that. Yes, we brought over the good stuff. Spirituality, fortitude, knowledge. Your dad wrote about that in *From the Middle Passage to the Inner City.*

TAYLOR: Yeah, yeah, yeah. Dad wrote about it. Whatever. When I try to point out the inequities, I'm told that I'm too angry or crazy, or it just isn't there.

DAD: But you know it's there, so . . .

TAYLOR: It's so perfectly set up to make us feel inferior.

DAD: You're letting people fuck with your mind, little girl. Don't give anyone that much power. Nobody can make you feel inferior. I've been the head of this house, coming to this island for the last forty

years, put in hundreds of thousands of dollars of renovations . . .
But there'll never be a sign out front that reads "LeVay." This will
always be the Whitcomb house, and I'll always be the guy lucky
enough to marry into the great Whitcomb dynasty . . . which for
a long time was a dynasty built on very little liquid money.

TAYLOR: Then you do understand.

DAD: I understand that you can be angry and not crazy. Just be a little
more . . . constructive.

TAYLOR: I just wish people would see it like I do.

DAD: Your daddy saw it.

TAYLOR: So what! He tells the white people, "You ain't shit." They give
him an award. "You still ain't shit." Another award. Meanwhile,
what changes?

DAD: Are you as hard on yourself as you are on your dad?

TAYLOR: Probably.

DAD: Your dad loved you.

TAYLOR: I'm not sure of that.

DAD: It's nature. We're programmed to love our kids.

[*Beat.*]

Breakfast?

TAYLOR: Thanks, no. I'm OK.

[KENT *enters from the side of the house.*]

DAD: Son.

KENT: Dad.

[DAD *exits to the kitchen. While* TAYLOR *and* KENT *talk on the porch,* DAD *searches through the fridge, makes himself breakfast, and sits down at the table to eat.*]

TAYLOR: It's really too bad you two have such a hard time.

KENT: Well, I worship him, like we're supposed to.

[*Long, uncomfortable pause.*]

TAYLOR:
Look, I really shouldn't have lit into her, or you . . . I was just . . . I don't know, you know?

KENT:
It was a mistake. The way I said what I was trying to say . . . I should have . . .

[*Long, uncomfortable pause.*]

TAYLOR:
It's hard when the stakes are all high and weird and then with your mom not here. I mean that was the whole point . . . right? For me to meet your mom. Right?

KENT:
I just really wanted you to meet Ma. And I admit, I admit I wanted them to like you . . . So I'm a little hypercritical and defensive and . . .

[*Long, uncomfortable pause.*]

TAYLOR:
I'm just trying to fit, you know . . .

KENT:
Don't try so hard, just be yourself.

[*Pause. Not uncomfortable. The air is clear.* CHERYL *enters the kitchen with small garbage bags from upstairs.*]

89

DAD: Hey Cheryl . . . I just used the last of the cream cheese, can you put that on the list?

CHERYL: What?

DAD: The shopping list?

CHERYL: You know what?

[CHERYL *begins to say something and then reconsiders.*]

No problem. Cream cheese.

[*She drops bags and exits to her bedroom.* TAYLOR *and* KENT *are still talking on the porch.*]

TAYLOR: So honey, where were you last night?

KENT: The Black Dog.

TAYLOR: All night?

KENT: No . . . I hung out with the tourists for a little while. The guest-house was locked . . . I slept on the boat. Here, got you a T-shirt.

TAYLOR: Thanks.

[CHERYL *returns to the kitchen with a small trash bag from her room. She struggles to collect all the bags to take them outside.*]

DAD: You need help?

CHERYL: No.

[*Scene switches to the porch.*]

KENT: She's our guest. And she hasn't done anything to you.

TAYLOR: Didn't we just make up? Really Spoon, I've had all the school-ing I can take. I'm sorry, I'll apologize, OK?

[*Long beat.* CHERYL *enters the porch with two garbage bags, walking to-ward the backyard, offstage. She can only walk through them, barely acknowledging* KENT *and ignoring* TAYLOR.]

KENT [*reaching for a bag*]: Here, let me . . .

CHERYL: No, I'm cool, but there's one more inside if you really want to . . .

TAYLOR: I'm gonna go on up and get dressed then . . .

KENT: I'll be up in a minute . . .

[CHERYL *exits off with bags.* TAYLOR *exits to the kitchen.* CHERYL *reap-pears from around the corner of the house, without garbage bags.*]

It's more fun when your mom's here. We haven't had any time to visit.

CHERYL: I know.

[*Scene switches to the kitchen.*]

TAYLOR: Thanks for lending the ear.

DAD: My pleasure. Listen, we can't control what others do.

TAYLOR: I know, I know. And we can't pick our families, and forgive-ness is good . . . Yeah, yeah, OK . . . I'm going up while there's still some hot water.

[TAYLOR *exits up the stairs. Scene switches to the porch.*]

KENT: You OK?

CHERYL: Yeah, I'm cool.

KENT: Worried about your ma?

CHERYL: No.

KENT: You need to talk?

CHERYL: Hell no.

KENT: You sure?

CHERYL: It's just . . . Mama called and . . . and . . . forget it.

KENT: Well, I'm here.

CHERYL: I hope so.

[Pause. CHERYL *hugs* KENT, *catching him off guard. She collects herself quickly.*]

You go on in. I got this.

KENT: So you're OK?

[TAYLOR *pokes her head into the kitchen.*]

TAYLOR: Doctor, uh . . . Joseph . . . I have a few things I need to rinse out . . . Should I ask Cheryl, or just pop them in the machine?

[*Beat.*]

You know what, forget it. I'll figure it out.

[*Scene switches to the porch.*]

CHERYL: Listen . . . I know this is the first time you brought somebody up here. She alright I guess . . . I might even like her if she'd just quit gettin' up under me when I'm tryin' to do my job.

KENT: She's just trying to fit in . . .

CHERYL: Tell her not to try so hard.

[*Beat.*]

At least she's black, kind of.

KENT: Kimber bothers you that much?

CHERYL: Yeah.

KENT: She's cool. She likes Flip.

CHERYL: I can't explain it.

[*Beat.*]

It hurts my feelings. It shouldn't, but it does.

[*Beat.*]

I've dated white boys.

KENT: You what?

CHERYL: I even liked some of them. What? Who was I supposed to date? The black boys at school, the ones like you and Flip? They weren't lining up to go out with a maid's daughter . . . Not one who doesn't put out.

KENT: Well, that's good. That you don't . . . Anyway . . .

CHERYL: Congratulations about your book. That's really nice. Seems like maybe what you should have been doing all along.

KENT: Yeah. Taylor helped me see that.

[*Long pause.*]

CHERYL: Well I better . . .

[KENT *picks up remaining trash bags and exits around the house.* CHERYL *exits into the kitchen, where she washes her hands in the sink, folds a stray dish towel, and exits to her room. Lights fade.*]


# SCENE 2

[*Later that morning. Outside* TAYLOR *lounges on the porch in a bikini top and shorts. She sips something cool, reads journals. A few moments later,* KENT *enters, also now fully dressed for the day. He sneaks behind* TAYLOR *and covers her eyes, planting a kiss on her neck.*]

TAYLOR: Kent?

KENT: What happened to Spoon? Of course it's me.

TAYLOR: Of course.

[*Beat.*]

You seem suspiciously happy.

KENT [*grinning*]: You could say that.

TAYLOR: What?

[*Beat.*]

What?

KENT: Got my galleys today.

TAYLOR: They sent them here?

KENT: Yeah . . . my editor gave the publisher the address . . . Anyway, here it is.

[KENT *hands the galleys to* TAYLOR.]

TAYLOR: Oh my God. Oh my God! This is it! Wow . . . Wow . . . It's gonna be right there, in the front . . . like at Barnes and Noble, Borders, hardcover fiction.

KENT: If it gets good reviews.

TAYLOR: It will!

KENT: I know.

TAYLOR: It's exciting.

KENT: I know.

TAYLOR [*flipping through pages*]: Where's the cover?

KENT: . . . Different department. It'll be nice. Read the dedication.

[KENT *flips to it. Pause while* TAYLOR *reads. She's moved.*]

TAYLOR: Really? Thank you. The love of your life, huh?

[*Beat.*]

Wow.

[DAD *and* FLIP *enter from the back of the house, carrying fishing poles and a pail.*]

DAD: Wow?

[KENT *takes galleys from* TAYLOR.]

KENT: You know Taylor, life excites her.

TAYLOR: OK then.

[*Beat.*]

You're going fishing?

DAD AND FLIP: Yeah.

[KIMBER *enters.*]

KIMBER: There you are.

TAYLOR: They're going fishing.

DAD: See, she catches on.

KIMBER: I didn't know you were a nature guy.

FLIP: I'm full of mystery and intrigue.

KENT: He's full of something.

DAD: We go out every summer, do some fishing, goof around, get away from the women. We throw back most of them.

FLIP: Yeah . . . just hang out on the boat, drink a little, shoot the shit. You should come.

KENT: Thanks . . . I've got work.

DAD: Work?

KENT: My book.

DAD: Oh . . . work.

KIMBER: I think I'll check out the shops today. Wanna come, Taylor?

TAYLOR: Really?

KIMBER: We'll be OK if we just talk about clothes and shoes—

TAYLOR: What about bags?

KENT: We can hang out here if you want, honey.

DAD: Thought you had work?

KENT: I do, but . . .

TAYLOR: I'll be fine. [*To* KIMBER] You won't make me go to Lilly Pulitzer or Kate Spade will you?

KIMBER: I thought you knew me better than that. Please.

KENT [*to* TAYLOR]: Here honey, take my card. Buy something pretty.

KIMBER: That's sweet.

[KIMBER *looks at* FLIP. *Beat.*]

FLIP: What?

KIMBER: OK then. We'll see you guys.

TAYLOR: I'll grab my purse and meet you round front.

[TAYLOR *and* KIMBER *exit.*]

DAD: Sons, ya done good. They're cute. Man, though, you've got a handful with that Taylor.

FLIP: Yeah, seems high-maintenance women is a family tradition. That's why I'm not even tryin' to—

KENT: Mom's not high maintenance. Is she?

DAD: No, no. Not if you keep your mouth shut, stay low, and keep the cash coming.

KENT: That doesn't seem fair.

[DAD *shrugs.*]

FLIP: Are we going? Come on, man, join us.

KENT: No really, I'm cool.

[DAD and FLIP start to exit.]

DAD: Did I tell you 'bout the time we went diving off the Ivory Coast? That water is so blue. I was snorkeling one day . . .

[DAD and FLIP exit. KENT watches them leave, takes the galleys out, and resumes his editing. Lights fade.]


SCENE 3

[LeVay house, early evening. KIMBER, FLIP, TAYLOR, and KENT lounge around a Scrabble board. Shopping bags are piled high near the front door.]

FLIP: Mojito . . . Twenty-three points!

TAYLOR: Fifteen.

FLIP: Look, that's a double letter. Mojito, mojito, mojito, mojito.

TAYLOR: It's a good drink. Maybe Cheryl can whip us up some tonight. Cheryl!

KENT: It's your spell.

TAYLOR: It's Spanish, right? Spanish or Mexican or something, right? Cheryl!

KIMBER: Taylor, your turn.

TAYLOR: Señor, ¿mo-hito, por favor?

KIMBER AND KENT: Spell!

[CHERYL *enters.*]

TAYLOR: There you are . . . I have a request.

FLIP: Ignore her, Cheryl.

TAYLOR: You think you could whip up some mojitos tonight? I would be much obliged.

[CHERYL *exits.*]

Wait, wait, wait . . . What is this? Pituitary. [*Spelling the word proudly*] P-i-t-u-i-t-a-r-y. All seven letters, and look at that, double word twice. Didn't know I had it in me did you? Didja? Right there, added it right onto p-i.

KIMBER [*to* KENT]: You'll have to cut her off, for the sake of the game.

TAYLOR: Pituitary! That's a gland.

KIMBER [*crossing to a chair, away from the game*]: This is useless.

TAYLOR: You're winning.

KIMBER: Look at my competition. You're all drunk. I'm out. No hard feelings?

TAYLOR: I just spelled "pituitary." You can't leave now.

FLIP: She did spell "pituitary."

TAYLOR: That is not the act of an inebriated woman.

KENT: Come on, baby.

KIMBER: I'm bored.

TAYLOR: Sure, it's a boring game. We play to win, not to have fun. I'm with Kimmy. Let's raise our glasses. To Kim-*ber*, my new best friend, for callin' it like it is. Pituitary or no pituitary.

[TAYLOR *finishes her drink with a flourish and curls onto the couch, her head in* KENT's *lap. He strokes her hair.* FLIP *lights a joint.*]

KENT: Ma isn't coming, is she?

FLIP: Sure as hell wouldn't be lighting up if I thought she was.

KENT: What do you think?

FLIP: Don't know. Tried to call her.

KENT: Me too. She's not picking up.

FLIP: If she's even there. I think they had a fight.

TAYLOR: It's deeper than that. Gotta be.

KIMBER: You should stay out of this.

TAYLOR: Are you telling me to—

KIMBER: Just a little womanly advice.

TAYLOR: OK. I'm gonna take that advice, because I may jes' be slightly alebrianated, anebreatated . . . And, you have great taste in shoes Kimbster.

[*Beat.*]

Can I tell you guys something?

KENT: Sure, honey.

TAYLOR: I think I'm gonna switch my focus to cockroaches. All that asthma inner-city kids have . . . that's dead roach dust.

KENT: That's great, honey.

TAYLOR: Yeah. Something a little more revelant. Relevant.

[KENT *passes on a drag but passes the joint to* KIMBER.]

FLIP: Maybe you're just burnt out chasing flies. I mean, this is your vacation and you've been running around with that butterfly net like something out of a D. H. Lawrence novel.

KIMBER: They collect bugs in D. H. Lawrence novels?

FLIP: Fine. A D. H. Lawrence movie. You know, with the rainbows and the lesbians and all lounging and the white dresses. [*To* KIMBER] You can pass that back now, sweetie.

[TAYLOR *rises and begins putting away the Scrabble board.*]

KIMBER: Why bugs anyway? Here you have this dad who's like the greatest sociologist of our time—

TAYLOR: Cultural anthropologist.

KIMBER: And what did your mom do?

KENT: Pan-Africanism.

TAYLOR: Politics and infrastructures.

KIMBER: And you go into bugs?

FLIP: Sometimes you just need to find your own way.

KENT: Look who's talking.

FLIP: Dad's a neurosurgeon; I do tits and faces.

TAYLOR: Actually it's related. In fifth grade my best friend didn't invite me to her birthday party.

KIMBER: You should probably let that go.

TAYLOR: It's anecdotal. Don't you remember the dividing point? You could play with anyone until like fifth grade, then it was over. Blacks over there, whites over here.

FLIP [*to* KIMBER]: You remember that, honey?

KIMBER: Yeah, actually I do.

KENT: Boys played sports. It didn't matter so much.

TAYLOR: Beyond Jack and Jill, there wasn't much at all to do once you were a teenager.

KIMBER: Jack and Jill?

KENT [*to* KIMBER]: Jack and Jill didn't let your people in.

TAYLOR: My people weren't so much welcome at Jack and Jill either.

FLIP: That's not true.

KIMBER: Jack and Jill?

[KIMBER *is ignored.*]

TAYLOR: Please? Lower middle class, single parent . . . uh-uh, wasn't gonna happen. Still, not my point. The party. I was heartbroken, and I didn't understand, and I guess Mom was damned if she was going to spell it out for me. So she was like . . . "Look, baby, you just have to look at everyone like they're bugs under a microscope. Like ants. Figure out the patterns."

FLIP: That sounds like a hippie, new-age, psycho Band-Aid.

KIMBER: What's Jack and Jill?

TAYLOR: Well, it worked. I mean, I look back and I'm damned if I know how you raise a little black girl around white privilege . . .

KIMBER: White anything . . .

TAYLOR: Yeah . . . and expect her to come out with some perspective. Some sense of self.

KIMBER: And it's getting worse.

FLIP: That's grim.

KIMBER: No, you read that paper I can't get published. You're not even allowed to say it's there anymore.

KENT: It?

KIMBER: Racism, discrimination, whatever. You can't imply that it exists. It's like we're supposed to have come so far that it's taboo to suggest we have any further to go.

TAYLOR: And I imagine these kids grow up thinking this intangible alienation is about them, right?

KIMBER: No. The kids I work with don't get what you got, because they don't even see white people. Theirs is more institutional, a lack of resources, a general lack of investment from anyone who could make a difference.

TAYLOR: OK, get this. So, I'm ten. I'm testing like college level on the verbal skills—

FLIP: She's such a show-off.

KENT: I like it in her.

TAYLOR: So I come home with this report card that says, attendance, superior; penmanship, outstanding; math skills, could use improvement; reading, satisfactory.

FLIP: What the hell kind of report card is that?

TAYLOR: A university lab school. Mommy hits the roof. And she's like, "Do you do the homework?" I do the homework. "Do you pay attention in class?" I pay attention. "Are you polite?" I'm polite. So we go to the school and she's hot. Really angry. And the teacher is like, "How is satisfactory a problem? Satisfactory is fine." And Mommy's like, "As far as I'm concerned, anything below above average for a child who's testing through the roof is a problem. The girl eats books for breakfast." And the teacher's still going, "We're very pleased with Taylor's work. It's always very good."

And finally, my mother says, "Look . . ." She stands right, and she's like, "Look, what do you have to do to make sure my child's working up to her potential every second of every day?" And the teacher looks at me and looks at Mommy and says, "But she is." And Mommy says, "Satisfactory is not Taylor's potential." And that was my last day at that school.

FLIP: Oh, you were homeschooled. That explains it.

KENT: The point is the teacher couldn't wrap her mind around black and above average coming in the same package.

TAYLOR: Thank you.

KIMBER: You were lucky.

TAYLOR: How do you figure?

KIMBER: OK. I get that your tale is supposed to be about the struggles to overcome adversity, or something. It's a bad example. The parent is supposed to be a working part of the school system, to facilitate change.

TAYLOR: Sure. But you're not hearing my point.

KIMBER: Yes. I do. I'm just saying that your example lacks heft.

TAYLOR: Heft.

KIMBER: The necessary weight to anchor your point.

[TAYLOR *rises.*]

TAYLOR: I know what heft is . . . Does anyone want something from the—

KIMBER: All I'm saying is that your example indicts a flawed school system.

TAYLOR: Flawed by institutional racism.

FLIP: She may have a point.

KENT: She definitely has a point.

KIMBER: She always has a point. But, for purposes of discussion, let's say you're the cutest, sweetest, prettiest little white girl in the school. In fact, let's make you Becky. [*To* TAYLOR] You're Becky and you've been blessed with the looks of some sort of Shirley Temple, young Elizabeth Taylor hybrid. And pretty much as long as you stay clean and smile at the teacher, which is easy because she's always smiling at you, and as long as you get along with your peers, which you do, because sadly, they've all been taught to value physical beauty above all else, and I'll even give you that you're good natured and passably intelligent. OK. I'll bet your parents won't question "satisfactory," if in fact they're in the country long enough to see your report card. Because it just doesn't matter, your destiny is decided, as long as you coast and don't fuck it up, you're fine.

TAYLOR: Because satisfactory is all Becky needs.

KIMBER: Because satisfactory is all that was ever expected of her.

KENT: I see where you're coming from.

TAYLOR: Look . . . Becky.

KIMBER: Oh, don't confuse us. I was never that pretty. And I was above average in verbal *and* math. My big sister was Becky. Oh my God, she had this cherubic beauty that matured into this ethereal beauty . . . and you couldn't touch her. You could only look, in awe. Mom spent a lot of time doing just that. She didn't have a chance. I believe that she had a deep and sensitive soul, and had never been equipped with the tools to nurture it. Hell, even to acknowledge it.

TAYLOR: So what, now the poor thing is married to some rich movie mogul and addicted to Xanax?

KIMBER: She killed herself at Prada.

[TAYLOR *laughs.*]

TAYLOR: That's not funny. I was right there until Prada.

KIMBER: You're right, it's not funny.

TAYLOR: You're kidding?

[*Beat.*]

You are kidding?

KIMBER: I wish. Two years ago my sister hanged herself in the dressing room. Daddy kept it out of the papers. You can imagine the store was more than happy to help.

TAYLOR: Wow.

KENT: Man.

FLIP: Jesus.

[*Long pause.*]

TAYLOR: Fine. You win. It's hard all around.

[TAYLOR *exits to the kitchen.*]

KENT: Man.

FLIP: You never told me about—

KIMBER [*smiling*]: Becky? Becky who?

[KIMBER *exits to the kitchen, where* TAYLOR *is absorbed with making a cup of tea. Scene changes to the kitchen.*]

TAYLOR: Guess those mojitos are never coming.

KIMBER: You shouldn't have asked for them.

TAYLOR: What?

KIMBER: It was disrespectful of Cheryl.

TAYLOR: I do nothing but try to help the girl and she's always surly as hell.

KIMBER: You're not supposed to help her. But you shouldn't treat her like a slave.

TAYLOR: Whoa . . .

KIMBER: I overstated. Still . . .

[TAYLOR *pauses.*]

TAYLOR: You're from Manhattan, right?

KIMBER: Yes.

TAYLOR: You fit in better here than I do.

KIMBER: The East Coast is it's own thing. Takes a little getting used to.

TAYLOR: No . . . it's this place specifically.

KIMBER: Sorry.

TAYLOR: It's OK. I'll learn. Or I'll be rejected and find a nice boy with a good pension.

KIMBER: You're so dramatic. Here, let me pour.

TAYLOR: I am sorry. About before.

KIMBER: Thank you. I didn't lose sleep over it. I get called a meddling rich bitch almost every day.

TAYLOR: It's good work that you do.

KIMBER: Thanks. I don't even care anymore if it's motivated by guilt. If more people felt guilty maybe we wouldn't be in this mess.

[TAYLOR *pours them tea.*]

TAYLOR: That was a good story. You had me for a second. You know, Prada sent it over the top.

KIMBER: I know. I couldn't resist.

[*Beat.*]

My sister lives. She is beautiful.

[*Beat.*]

She's married to a movie mogul and addicted to Xanax.

[*Long pause.*]

What's Jack and Jill?

TAYLOR: An organization for elite black kids and teenagers. They go to museums, trips abroad . . . sometimes the teenagers have coming-out cotillions and . . .

KIMBER: Thank you. One more question.

[*Beat.*]

When did you two? . . .

TAYLOR: He told you?

[*Beat.*]

A long time ago, it was nothing. I don't think he deserves you.

KIMBER: You're so out of line with that. I don't think you deserve Kent. He really loves you, you know. It's hard to find someone who will love you like that.

[CHERYL *enters the kitchen holding a small book.*]

CHERYL: Far as I'm concerned they're both too good for both of you. I went to find the bartending manual. For your mojitos.

TAYLOR: I'm sorry, Cheryl, I shouldn't have—

CHERYL: It's OK. [*Looking in the book*] We don't have fresh mint anyway.

TAYLOR: Oh.

CHERYL: Or limes.

KIMBER: It's OK.

CHERYL: Or rum.

[*There's a moment of silence. All see the humor in the moment.*]

TAYLOR: Sit down, Cheryl. Let me get you some tea.

CHERYL: That's OK.

KIMBER: Oh, just do it.

[*Beat.*]

It's a girl thing.

[*The phone rings and* KIMBER *gets it.*]

Hello. Oh, hi, Mrs., uh, Ellie. Sure. She's right here.

[KIMBER *hands* CHERYL *the phone and takes a tea service from the cabinet. Both busy themselves while* CHERYL *talks.*]

CHERYL: Ma . . . Yeah.

[*Beat.*]

I can't talk about it anymore. I don't know. I don't know. No, I haven't talked to him yet.

TAYLOR: Is everything OK?

[CHERYL *moves to a corner, with her back to the room.*]

CHERYL: I'm in the kitchen.

[*Beat.*]

With people.

[*Pause.*]

OK.

KIMBER: What do you think of chai?

TAYLOR: Highly overrated. I like the basics . . . Earl Grey, English breakfast, Darjeeling . . .

KIMBER: A fan of the colonialists, are you?

CHERYL [*yelling*]: . . . Ma, I have to go!

[KENT *and* FLIP *enter the kitchen.*]

KENT: Just wanted to make sure you hadn't killed each other.

FLIP: If you're gonna fight, could you take off your shirts first?

CHERYL [*on the phone*]: Why do you keep pushing?

TAYLOR: Ssshh, Cheryl's on the phone.

KIMBER: Want tea, honey?

FLIP: I'm a man. Do I look like I want tea?

[*Beat.*]

Do we have Sleepytime?

CHERYL [*yelling*]: Stop . . . Stop! I can't do this!

[*Pause.* CHERYL *hangs up the phone.*]

KENT: Cheryl?

TAYLOR: Are you crying?

KENT [*to* CHERYL]: What's wrong?

CHERYL: I'm fine.

FLIP: OK. You know if we have Sleepytime?

CHERYL: You know what. I'm done. You can kiss my ass is what you can do with your tea.

TAYLOR: Cheryl?

[TAYLOR *goes over to* CHERYL *and puts her hand on her shoulder.*]

CHERYL: Don't touch me.

[CHERYL *backs up.* KENT *approaches her, intending to comfort her.*]

. . . Back off. Get. All of you. Back the fuck up. Oh my God. Oh my God . . . I can't breathe. I can't . . . Oh my God. Oh my . . . Oh my God . . .

[CHERYL *is hyperventilating. She puts her hands on her knees.*]

I can't . . . Oh God . . . What's happening to me?

FLIP: Taylor, get a paper bag.

KIMBER [*to* FLIP]: She's hyperventilating.

[KIMBER *rubs* CHERYL'S *back.*]

You're OK, Cheryl. Breathe . . . Breathe . . .

[TAYLOR *rolls up the bag and helps* CHERYL *breathe into it.*]

It's going to be OK now. It is . . .

KENT: Should I call 911?

FLIP: No. No. She'll be OK.

CHERYL: Mama asked me to ask him . . . and I did . . . I went to Dr. LeVay and asked if he had something to say . . . and . . . Oh God . . .

TAYLOR: Just breathe . . . you don't have to . . .

CHERYL: And Mrs. LeVay's steady calling . . . wants to talk to Dr. LeVay, and he won't . . . It's crazy. And you two didn't know?

FLIP: I still don't know what the hell's going on.

CHERYL: Then you're slow.

[*At that moment* DAD *enters from outside.*]

DAD: Boys . . . I need you to look at the storm windows . . .

[*Silence.*]

What's up?

CHERYL: I know Dr. LeVay. I know everything.

DAD: Maybe we should talk about this, alone.

CHERYL: No! No! No!

[KIMBER *starts to walk out of the kitchen.*]

[*To* KIMBER] Stay here. [*To* FLIP *and* KENT] And how the hell didn't not one of you sorry mothafuckas not figure it out . . . Because you don't think 'bout nothin' but yourselves and your damn socioeconomic bantering, and bugs, and relationship dysfunction and shit.

KENT: Is this about your mom?

CHERYL: No! Yes . . . And I don't know what the hell she's thinkin' sendin' me up here like this . . .

KENT: Hey, hey, hey . . . slow down . . . start from the beginning.

CHERYL: Shut up. Seriously the most self-involved, bullshit people.

[*Beat.*]

Mrs. LeVay found out. She came home and told that man that she knew he was my daddy. Then she kicked your ass out the house, didn't she, Dr. LeVay? And he brings his sorry ass up here. So you knew and you looked me in the face and said, "You know how I like my sandwiches," or some shit like that.

FLIP: Dad?

CHERYL: That's right. *Dad!* OK. OK.

[*Long pause.*]

So, two weeks ago . . . One of Mrs. LeVay's "friends" invites her to sit on the board at the high school where I'm supposed to be on scholarship, right? It's a big ole lunch in some sort of fancy oak-paneled room . . . This is how it got told to my mama, anyway. You know there's a network of maids . . . they talk . . . So, the ladies who lunch are lunching, and this woman says, "Michelle, it's so generous what your husband has been doing for that girl all these years."

DAD: Cheryl—

CHERYL [*continuing*]: Eighteen years . . . you can keep your mouth shut for five more minutes . . . Imagine it . . . you could smell the money, all those skinny rich bitches staring at her over their shrimp salads. "Four years now, right, Michelle?" Mrs. LeVay's been set up. Your Daddy's been paying my tuition there since I started. Fought to have me accepted but insisted it remain on the DL. [*To* KIMBER] That's down low. Twenty-five thousand a year. So, this is the thing that's the craziest. It wasn't that Mrs. LeVay was broken up about a kid who shares her own kids' gene pool washing her crusty sheets. No, the tragedy was that it got out. She calls my mother, threatens to fire her . . . calls her all out of her name, after Ma's been so quiet about it all these years . . . and threatens to take us to court for libel. I'm supposed to have a daddy got shot in the Gulf . . . And you knew . . . how can you live with yourself?

[CHERYL *runs off to her room. All stare at* DAD, *speechless.* KENT *sits down.* FLIP *paces.* DAD *looks at them all.*]

FLIP: Say it's not true, Dad . . . Say it . . . Daddy, please. She's lying, isn't she? Tell me that she's lying . . . She's lying.

[*Pause.*]

OK ... OK ... gimme a second. OK ... I guess I can see how it could happen, right? Mom's a little chilly one night, Ms. Ellie's down here looking, I don't know, however she looked thirty pounds ago, a little flour on her forehead maybe. But tell me how you did not stop to think about us? While we were sleeping upstairs, you came down here and had your way with the maid? How did you not think about us? Shit.

[DAD *and* FLIP *square off.* DAD *backs up, turns around, exits kitchen, and then exits out the front door. Lights fade.*]

## SCENE 4

[*Following morning, in the kitchen.* CHERYL, FLIP, KIMBER, KENT, *and* TAYLOR *sit at the breakfast table. They eat in silence. A very long silence. The toaster pops up.* TAYLOR *gets up to get it.*]

TAYLOR: Butter?

| CHERYL AND KENT: | KIMBER AND FLIP: |
|---|---|
| Yes. | No. |

[TAYLOR *serves toast and sits back down.*]

TAYLOR: Orange juice?

KENT AND FLIP: Sure.

CHERYL: I'd like more coffee. Please. So, none of you all have nothing to say?

FLIP: I'd like some juice.

[TAYLOR *serves. They resume, in silence. Long pause.*]

CHERYL: None of you all have nothin' to say?

FLIP: "Anything." We don't have anything to say, Cheryl.

KIMBER: Flip.

FLIP: What. What am I supposed to say? Congratulations, it's a girl! Welcome to the family! Glad I didn't seduce you last Christmas!

CHERYL: It's cool. I'm not even trying to be a part of this family. I have a family.

FLIP: So you don't lay claim on any of Dad's money?

CHERYL: I didn't say that.

KENT [*to* FLIP] Apologize to her!

FLIP: For what? Oh no . . . there's gonna be some blood work done up in here 'fore I'm apologizing to anyone.

KENT: Well, I'm sorry, Cheryl. I'm so sorry. And I think I knew somehow . . . not really, just kind of felt . . .

TAYLOR: Except it's fucked because you all let her clean up your shit.

CHERYL: I didn't touch nobody's shit. Why you always want to make what I do shameful?

TAYLOR: I'm on your side.

CHERYL: No you're not. You spend the whole weekend up under me, apologizing to me, for me, overthanking me . . . like what I do embarrasses you.

TAYLOR: I'm sorry, Cheryl.

CHERYL: I do good, honest work that helps people. You think studying the mating habits of the South Seas blue-eyed friggin' fly is more useful?

TAYLOR: I didn't say . . .

[*Beat.*]

CHERYL: You just need to understand that I'm more a part of this family than you'll ever be. I've had a room in this house, in Aspen, and New York for as long as I've been alive. I think you've confused me for you. We're very different, Taylor. I'm not trying to find my place . . . this is my home.

[FLIP *gets up.*]

FLIP: Well, on that note . . .

[FLIP *exits.* KENT *gets up to follow.*]

TAYLOR [*to* KENT]: Where you going?

KENT: Away.

[KENT *exits the kitchen. In the living room,* FLIP *pours a drink.* KENT *sits with his head in his hands.* FLIP *hands* KENT *his drink and pours himself another.*]

It's all so crazy . . . but on some level I'm starting to understand . . .

FLIP: You're blowin' my mind if you're about to give Dad a pass on this one.

KENT: No. No. It's awful. Really, really, like Jerry-fuckin'-Springer insane. I just keep thinking of all the stories. How Daddy couldn't stay in the dorms, or walk in the yard after sundown. How Daddy wasn't allowed to make his valedictorian speech, or do his residency at Boston. How he got his ass kicked when those guys thought Mom was white. Wouldn't all that make you crazy? Wouldn't that make you want to stake a claim on anything you could lay your hands on? Shit, even now he can't play golf where his colleagues do.

FLIP: Dad doesn't play golf.

KENT: And why not, do you suppose?

[*Beat.*]

Here's the thing. All this time, all these years, I've been running up under you two. Hating myself because I have no desire to kill deer, or climb mountains, or rate pussy. Dad taught us both that there was something wrong with me for that. And I believed it. I'm fifteen and all I want, just like every other fifteen-year-old boy, is to have a cute girl like me, maybe get to second base . . . but I'm thinkin' I can't because I've got some sort of, I don't know, testosterone deficiency. My daddy made me think that. Why? Because I give a shit about people? Because I don't put myself first? Because I hear what women say, and actually like them for it? I admire the hell out of you, Flip. I do. You the man. I just wanted you to think the same about me.

FLIP: Kent, I never said—

KENT: Save it. It doesn't matter. It really doesn't. Dad doesn't like me because he doesn't like himself. But it doesn't matter. That's his cross. I'm done.

[*Scene switches to the kitchen.*]

TAYLOR: Be honest, you weren't even trying to like me.

CHERYL: It wasn't my job to like you.

TAYLOR: I wasn't apologizing for you . . . I never had a cleaning lady. You all have all these rules . . . these invisible lines . . . all this tension flying around, and I'm just trying to meet the new family. Right? Truly, I am sorry if I insulted you.

CHERYL: You didn't insult me. Mostly you just irritate me. But you do get that you're not at the top of my list at the moment?

KIMBER: She's apologizing, Cheryl . . .

CHERYL: And you . . . you . . .

KIMBER: Stop. Before you say it, just stop.

CHERYL: You don't deserve him.

KIMBER: Honey, I'm sorry, but he's off the table for you anyway.

[*Scene switches to the living room.*]

KENT: Are you crying?

FLIP: No.

[FLIP *moves away and faces the back wall.*]

KENT: All he had to do was keep it in his pants for five minutes.

FLIP: All he had to do was respect us enough to keep it in his pants at home.

KENT: Respect us? What about respect Ma?

FLIP: They have an arrangement.

KENT: No they don't.

FLIP: Dad told me. It's an understanding; they don't even have to say it. You marry a real man, that's what you get. She knows that. The deal is, he treats her well, keeps his shit in the street away from the rumor mill, and they're cool.

KENT: That's bullshit.

FLIP: No . . . bullshit is Dad screwing Ms. Ellie.

[*Scene switches to the kitchen.*]

KIMBER: So did he know?

TAYLOR: He had to—

CHERYL: I have to believe he didn't, not right away.

[*Scene switches to the living room.*]

KENT: It amazes me you have no thought for Ma in all this.

FLIP: . . . She made her bed.

KENT: Your whole worldview is seriously [*searching for word*] skewed.

FLIP: I know you're Ma's favorite . . . but you can't see how she is?

KENT: He ignored her, Flip. He screwed around with anything in a skirt . . . and she knew it.

FLIP: Ma went slummin'. She went slumming, got what she was shopping for, and spent the rest of their lives punishing Dad for it. You were too young, you didn't see it. Ma can be a—

KENT: Take it back!

FLIP: Take it back? What are you, twelve?

KENT: If, if she was a . . . If she was . . . It's because he humiliated her. It was cruel. It was wrong. And if he's really got you convinced that's the rules, you're gonna be fucked . . . Or I guess you'll marry some poor passive white girl with self-esteem issues and torture her.

FLIP: Kimber is not passive.

KENT: Yeah, but you're not smart enough to marry her.

FLIP: Fuck you.

KENT: Get some help!

[KENT *walks across the room.* FLIP *refills his glass. Scene switches to the kitchen.*]

CHERYL: I feel like I don't exist.

TAYLOR: I know how you feel.

CHERYL: No you don't. Jesus, your dad's famous . . . That's a free pass to anywhere you wanna go. I'm bustin' my ass trying to raise enough money to supplement work-study, and you cryin' in your milk because people at Harvard were mean to you.

KIMBER: I've seen that kind of mean, it's crazy.

CHERYL: You think people at that stuck-up school weren't mean to me? Of course they were, and it wasn't just the white girls. They were all mean. But I didn't lose sleep over it. Because I knew who I was before I got there.

TAYLOR: Oh, you're pretty well adjusted, huh?

CHERYL: Yes.

TAYLOR: Well who are you now?

[*Silence.*]

That's all I'm saying. It's a little blurry, huh? I'm thinking maybe your mother did you a service.

[*Scene switches to the living room.*]

FLIP: Maybe he didn't know. It's possible. Remember, Ellie went away for a year and came back with the baby and that picture of her dead husband.

KENT: OK. So they do their thing, eight months later there's a baby . . . You serious?

FLIP: She trapped him.

KENT: Oh yeah. Ms. Ellie, the original whoring church lady sets a diabolical trap, and then, just to show him, works as a maid for eighteen years.

FLIP: I've had church ladies . . . They can be freaks—

KENT: You're sick.

FLIP: No. I'm my father's son.

[*Silence.*]

KENT: You slept with her, didn't you?

FLIP: She told you?

KENT: She told me she's a virgin.

FLIP: You believed that?

KENT: Why not?

FLIP: So you two haven't . . . ?

KENT: No. Hell no.

FLIP: It was a long time ago . . . I'm sorry . . . I wasn't gonna tell you.

KENT: She's only eighteen.

FLIP: Who are we talking about?

KENT: Cheryl.

FLIP: You think I'm a child molester?

KENT: Wait a minute . . . You're talking about . . . Oh . . . Oh shit . . . No . . .

FLIP: Man it was nothing—

[KENT *punches him. It's quick and clean. It's over. Scene switches to the kitchen.*]

TAYLOR: Why would she stay on?

CHERYL: Says it was the only way she could think to make sure I got the experiences I was owed. So, I can ski. And snorkel. And ride horses. English and western . . . I suppose with that, the world should lay itself at my feet.

KIMBER: That's cultural capital.

CHERYL: Well, it don't help nothin'.

TAYLOR: Couldn't she have just—

CHERYL: I am so through talking about this . . . Please.

[*Scene switches to the living room.*]

FLIP: Man. I'm sorry. It was years ago. And I was lying when I said it was nothing. I was too fucked up to know that. You're better for her.

KENT: I know.

[FLIP *starts to head upstairs.*]

FLIP: You gonna be OK?

KENT: Eventually. Just get out.

[KENT *sits on the couch. In the kitchen,* KIMBER *rises and begins clearing the table.* TAYLOR *joins her.* CHERYL *flips absently through a magazine. Long pause.*]

CHERYL: I do hate that you're with him.

TAYLOR: Why?

CHERYL: Not you, Miss It's-all-about-me-girl . . . Damn . . . [*To* KIMBER] You.

KIMBER: Oh . . . I hadn't noticed.

CHERYL: . . . OK. So, 'splain this to me. You white, right?

KIMBER: Right.

CHERYL: And you trade in to be black?

KIMBER: Yeah, I'd not be inclined to take a pass on white privilege.

TAYLOR: I'm happy being black.

CHERYL: Did I ask you?

KIMBER: We did draw the short end of the stick on aging.

CHERYL: Yeah, that's true. So why you like our men so much?

KIMBER: Did I say I like your men? No. I like your . . . I like Flip. I love Flip. This is really what you want to talk about, right now? Really? Today?

CHERYL: Clearly I'm workin' through some things . . .

KIMBER: OK. So yes, Flip's fine . . . the way only a fine black man can be fine. Of course I like that. But people want to think it's just that . . . which is just, insulting on so many levels I can't even begin. And I get it, I do . . . I get why it would piss off black women, or white men. But it can't be my problem. All I can do is understand it, and sit in it. But I won't apologize. You'd be insulted if I did.

CHERYL: Blonde and pretty opens a lot of doors, but you'd want to have brown babies? Why?

KIMBER: I want to have the babies of the man I love. They'll come out whatever color they come out, and I will love them because they will be my babies. You can't know this. But you will. You will be in love one day, and you will know this.

CHERYL: Well, at least you're pretty.

[*Pause.*]

TAYLOR: Also . . . black men are almost never serial killers, they dress well, and usually can dance.

CHERYL: Damn . . . I'm tryin' so hard to not like you . . . but you're so strange, I almost can't help it.

TAYLOR: It's part of my charm.

[*Moment of silence.* CHERYL *chooses to be amused. Lights fade.*]


# SCENE 5

[*Later that afternoon. Downstairs empty. Several stacks of suitcases are piled by the door.* CHERYL *stands on the back porch. She opens one of* TAYLOR's *jars after another and lets the flies out.* DAD *enters from the side of the house.*]

CHERYL: I thought you'd be gone a long time ago.

DAD: I would have . . .

[CHERYL *breaks down.* DAD *goes to her. He takes her into his arms. She sobs for a moment, and then pushes him away. She stands with her back to him. He gives her his handkerchief.*]

Look . . . I didn't know . . . not until four years ago when your mother asked me to set up a trust fund . . . I couldn't, not without it all coming out . . . I got overwhelmed . . . I said the wrong things . . . made the wrong choices.

CHERYL: That makes it worse.

DAD: I don't have anything else to say.

CHERYL: You don't have anything else to say? That's it? Four years . . . Eighteen years . . . What's the difference . . . ? Once you knew, you didn't want me?

[CHERYL *goes through kitchen into living room;* DAD *follows.*]

DAD: It's more complicated than that . . .

CHERYL: You didn't recognize me?

DAD: What?

CHERYL: Eighteen years ago . . . I was a baby. I've seen the pictures . . . I was cute.

[TAYLOR *comes down the stairs with the last of her things and an empty crate for her jars. They do not notice her.*]

I was really cute. And you couldn't see me, and love me, and want me? How come you couldn't see yourself in my eyes? How come you couldn't feel like you was put here to protect me? How they rate? But I just didn't matter? And you still don't see me. Me. Me. Your daughter. The first man who loves you is supposed to be your father. You were supposed to love me first. And best. And how can anyone ever love me right if you couldn't love me first? And I'm thinkin' I'm mad at the white girl, 'cause she took my men . . . but she didn't . . . they just don't see me. And I'm thinkin' I don't like Taylor 'cause she trying so hard to be seen. But I don't like her 'cause she like me. She got the same . . . holes in her. But all this time, it was you. I deserve to be seen.

[*Long silence.*]

DAD: I don't know what you want.

CHERYL: Then I feel sorry for you.

TAYLOR: She wanted you to say, "I'm sorry . . . I love you . . . I'm here for you."

[*A long silence.*]

DAD: I really should be going.

TAYLOR: Just tell me one thing. How do you do that? How do men make babies and then just, disregard them.

DAD: We don't all . . .

TAYLOR: Please. How is it someone who's supposed to be a genius, who's supposed to have such a capacity for understanding the workings of the human mind, could treat family like this? What kind of sickness lets you just cut the inconvenient pieces out. I just want to know.

DAD: You're not talking about me, Taylor.

TAYLOR: Sure I am. My dad is gone. I never got to ask him. But here you are, and I think I really need you to help me understand.

CHERYL: I think you should answer her. I think it's the least you could do.

DAD: I guess you really don't feel the shit until it hits the fan.

[KENT *enters.*]

KENT: That's the best you can do? You don't feel the shit till it hits the fan? . . . What kind of—

TAYLOR: I don't understand.

DAD: I don't know, sweetheart. It has something to do with manhood and self-preservation, and struggling to prove yourself all the time.

KENT: Prove what . . . ? It's your house.

DAD: It's your mother's house.

TAYLOR: So you just . . . pretend? For eighteen years?

DAD: Four—

KENT: Years, Dad.

DAD: I could do better than pretend. I could make it not so just by deciding. Ellie never complained, Cheryl. You never wanted for a roof over your head. I got her into the best high school in the country, that'll set her up for the rest of her life . . .

KENT: That's bullshit . . .

DAD [to KENT]: Have you lost your mind?

TAYLOR: Don't go. Stay and make it better.

DAD: It won't get better. We'll just become resigned to it. Maybe your mother will divorce me first, but I doubt it. Divorce is worse than martyrdom. She'll get a lot of sympathy; I'll give her a lot of jewelry. You looked at me lately? I'm still a pretty good-looking date to the opera.

[FLIP *and* KIMBER *have entered the living room, unnoticed. They too carry luggage.*]

TAYLOR: Just stay.

DAD: I'm not your dad, Taylor.

FLIP: Verdict's still out on that one.

[*Beat.*]

Dad.

TAYLOR: You're leaving now too?

FLIP: Yeah. [*To* DAD] I'm surprised you're still here.

TAYLOR: You all need to stay!

DAD, FLIP, AND KENT: Why?

TAYLOR: To clean up the mess.

FLIP: We hire people for that, Taylor.

TAYLOR: How's that working for you?

FLIP [*to* KENT]: Can you make her shut up?

KENT: Leave it, Taylor. Please.

TAYLOR: Please don't leave me—

KENT: Taylor. Leave it.

TAYLOR: I'm just saying—

KENT: I'm just saying . . . [*Yelling*] Stop. Just stop!

TAYLOR: I can't lose another one . . . please . . . don't go.

KENT [*yelling*]: It's not your fight!

TAYLOR: No. It's yours. So fight it. Fight this one yourself then . . . [*To* DAD] Please stay.

KENT: Sweetie . . . you have to be quiet now . . . you must . . . shhhhh sshhhh.

[KENT *pulls* TAYLOR *into his embrace and soothes her.*]

DAD: Nicely handled, son . . . Didn't know you had it in you.

FLIP: That's what you're gonna do? Criticize Kent. Right now?

[*Beat.*]

You amaze me.

DAD: We're cut from the same cloth.

FLIP: You're wrong.

DAD: Yes, son, about some things. Not about that.

FLIP: You use that word, "son," like a trump card. That's not affection; that's a power play.

DAD: That's all you get! [*Yelling*] That's all you get! I settled down, raised two bright sons, supported a high-maintenance woman at the level to which she was accustomed. What do you do? Spend money fast as you can make it and sleep your way through Atlanta society? Sounds empty. Yeah, we're cut from the same cloth, but I grew up.

[*Beat.*]

You want to apologize?

FLIP: No.

DAD: There isn't a single one of you that hasn't kept secrets or made mistakes. So you kids think carefully if you want to start throwing stones up in this house. Pretty much from the second they bring you ingrates home from the hospital, every waking moment is spent trying to keep your asses safe and provided for. [*To* FLIP] Are your teeth straight? I did that. [*To* KENT] Did you get any degree from any school that you wanted? I followed the rules. I worked hard. I supported the household. I gave you everything. You are equipped. [*To* CHERYL] Even you. That was my time, my money, my choices. I tell you what, you go out there and find me a man who hasn't made mistakes, then you judge.

[*Long silence.* DAD *crosses to the whiskey. Pours himself a drink, downs it. Long pause.*]

KENT: But Daddy, it doesn't make it OK.

[KENT *exits to the kitchen.* TAYLOR *follows.*]

KIMBER: Should I start loading the car?

FLIP: I'll get it, baby.

[*Scene switches to the kitchen.*]

TAYLOR: I'm sorry . . .

KENT: About? . . .

TAYLOR: Everything.

[*Scene switches to the living room.*]

KIMBER: Thank you for your hospitality, Dr. LeVay.

DAD: That's funny. I tell you what. See if you can't make this boy do right by you. He doesn't know it, but he needs you.

KIMBER: Yes, sir.

[FLIP *exits to the car with bags. Scene switches to the kitchen.*]

TAYLOR: Nothing happened with Flip this weekend that's worth mentioning. But six years ago . . .

KENT: I know.

TAYLOR: And you'll stay with me?

KENT: Life's going to be a lot easier, for both of us, if you'll just accept that I'm not leaving. Ever.

[*Beat.*]

But I am going upstairs . . . for a second. . . I'll be back.

[KENT *exits, running toward stairs past* FLIP, DAD, KIMBER *and* CHERYL.]

DAD: I'm sorry for the fireworks. Come back at Christmas and we'll be back to our usual levels of mirthful dysfunction.

[*They all stand awkwardly.*]

FLIP [*to* KIMBER]: Let's give your folks a call, huh?

KIMBER: OK.

FLIP: Maybe even pick up a hostess gift on the way?

KIMBER: Yeah . . . uh, sure. Great.

[KIMBER *gestures to* FLIP *to speak with* DAD.]

FLIP [*to* DAD]: You scheduled a flight out?

DAD: Yeah.

FLIP: Want a lift to the airport?

DAD: Thanks.

[KENT *comes down the stairs.* TAYLOR *has entered the living room. They all stand in area in front of doors.*]

KENT: Wait. Dad. Wait.

DAD: Son?

KENT: I want you to read this, OK?

DAD: You're giving me your book.

KENT: Yeah. It's not a peace offering. It's something I need to do, for me. But don't call me about it if you don't like it. In fact, don't call me at all. But I poured a few years of my life into it, and the publisher thinks it'll do well, and I thought you should have it early.

[*Beat.*]

It's good.

KIMBER: Well, I'll meet you guys in the car. Thanks for everything. It was nice meeting you, Taylor.

TAYLOR [*from the stairs*]: Yeah, you too.

KIMBER: Cheryl.

CHERYL: Take care.

DAD: OK then.

[DAD *looks at* CHERYL, *starts toward her and then backs away. He shoulders his duffle bag. And, without looking back, walks out of the door.*]

CHERYL: Well that sucked.

TAYLOR: Yeah.

CHERYL: OK. Well, I'm 'bout done with all y'all. I'm going to pack. You all will have to shut the house down best you can. Kent, you'll give me a ride to the ferry?

KENT: Sure.

CHERYL [*to* TAYLOR]: Be nice to him, OK? He's like family to me.

TAYLOR: Of course I will. He's the love of my life.

[CHERYL *and* TAYLOR *hug.* CHERYL *exits to her bedroom.* KENT *looks out the door, closes it, and stands in the foyer, stunned.* TAYLOR *walks down to him. They embrace.*]

Do you think they liked me?

Kent (Daniel J. Bryant) and Taylor (Ann Joseph) meet at Dr. James Bradley
Scott's funeral.

Kent (Bryant; *center*) pays attention to his "calcium intake" as Flip (Aaron Todd Douglas) and Dad (Phillip Edward Van Lear) talk.

Dad (Van Lear) eats pickled pigs' feet and shares a moment with Cheryl (Ericka Ratcliff) in the kitchen.

A moment on the porch with Taylor (Joseph) and her flies.

Kimber (Anne Roche) charms the crowd.

*Left to right:* Kimber (Roche), Cheryl (Ratcliff), and Taylor (Joseph) stare at Dad in disbelief.

"Quality family time." *Left to right:* Kent (Bryant), Taylor (Joseph), Kimber (Roche), Cheryl (Ratcliff), Flip (Douglas), and Dad (Van Lear).

Kent (Bryant; *fourth from left*) gives his manuscript to Dad (Van Lear; *third from left*) as the family prepares to leave the Vineyard. *Left to right:* Kimber (Roche), Flip (Douglas), Cheryl (Ratcliff), and Taylor (Joseph) watch.